Praise for *Focused Fundraising*

"This book tackles a topic—instant overload due to too much to do, too many distractions, and too little time—that is affecting everyone. Focusing on the important over the urgent is not always easy and Michael and Chris present tactics and some big-picture thinking that help fundraisers and the nonprofit sector. This book is full of strategies that I can use with my team."

—**Theresa A. Pesch,**
President and VP of Philanthropy,
Hennepin Healthcare Foundation

"*Focused Fundraising* provides advancement professionals with tips and tricks that can help cut through the noise. Chris and Michael present step-by-step guides to deal with the daily grind and help you target what matters most."

—**Donald J. Whelan,** Jr.,
Vice Chancellor, University of Advancement,
Texas Christian University

"In a remote/hybrid fundraising world, we all need fresh ways to prioritize, plan, and manage. *Focused Fundraising* is your essential playbook for navigating these uncertain times."

—**Eugénie I. Gentry,**
Yale University for Humanity Campaign Director,
Associate Vice President for Development

"We always get the results of our choices. *Focused Fundraising's* common-sense approach challenges us to move beyond our old habits and make better choices of what we focus on."

—**Alan Fine,**
author, *You Already Know How To Be Great*

"Nonprofit work and fundraising requires daily inspiration so you can stay focused on what really matters, be resilient in the face of setbacks, and steadily move your vision and goals forward. With this book in hand, you've got a key resource to keep you motivated and on track."

—**Allison A. Holzer,**
co-author of *Dare to Inspire: Sustain the Fire of Inspiration in Work and Life,*
Master Certified Coach and co-CEO of InspireCorps

FOCUSED
FUNDRAISING

HOW TO RAISE YOUR SIGHTS AND OVERCOME OVERLOAD

CHRISTOPHER M. CANNON
MICHAEL FELBERBAUM

WILEY

Published by John Wiley & Sons, Inc., Hoboken, New Jersey.
Published simultaneously in Canada.

For general information on our other products and services or for technical support, please contact our Customer Care Department within the United States at (800) 762-2974, outside the United States at (317) 572-3993 or fax (317) 572-4002.

Wiley also publishes its books in a variety of electronic formats. Some content that appears in print may not be available in electronic formats. For more information about Wiley products, visit our web site at www.wiley.com.

Library of Congress Cataloging-in-Publication Data:

Names: Cannon, Christopher M., author. | Felberbaum, Michael (Director), author.
Title: Focused fundraising / Christopher M Cannon, Michael Felberbaum.
Description: Hoboken, New Jersey : Wiley, [2022] | Includes bibliographical references and index.
Identifiers: LCCN 2022011364 (print) | LCCN 2022011365 (ebook) | ISBN 9781119835271 (cloth) | ISBN 9781119835295 (adobe pdf) | ISBN 9781119835288 (epub)
Subjects: LCSH: Fund raising.
Classification: LCC HG177 .C366 2022 (print) | LCC HG177 (ebook) | DDC 658.15/224—dc23/eng/20220603
LC record available at https://lccn.loc.gov/2022011364
LC ebook record available at https://lccn.loc.gov/2022011365

Cover Image: © VectorHot/Getty Images
Cover Design: Wiley

SKY10034447_071222

Contents

Welcome to *Focused Fundraising: How to RAISE Your Sights and Overcome Overload*

IF YOU HAVE spent any time working or volunteering for a nonprofit organization, you know the constant craziness. Running 24/7 seems like the only option. With so much going on, is focus even possible?

The answer is an emphatic "Yes!" We have seen focus take hold at nonprofits large and small. And when overloaded individuals and teams finds focus, amazing things can happen.

You hold in your hands a vital resource to help you and your organization focus. Focus asks a lot every moment of every day, especially considering there is not a single nonprofit professional or volunteer we have met who isn't overloaded. That is why this book is about gaining focus amidst overload. With trusted tools and an open mindset, you can raise your sights and overcome overload. And so can your organization. *Focused Fundraising* will help you get there.

There are countless books to help you win your next solicitation or structure your next fundraising campaign. We wrote *Focused Fundraising* because, if you are like most of the professionals and volunteers we surveyed and interviewed, your biggest challenge is not fundraising technique—your challenge is finding time. Finding time to think. Finding time to plan and build for the future. Finding time to be there for your donors. Finding time for yourself.

Only you can bring what you bring to causes you care about. No matter where you work in the nonprofit fundraising process, nor how long you have been involved in nonprofit life, *Focused Fundraising* is your playbook to thrive in the constant craziness.

Focused Fundraising started pre-pandemic. Way back in 2019, when emails were too plentiful and social media choices were growing by the day (you know, pre-TikTok but post-Instagram), we recognized that distraction plagued our profession. We were constantly on the brink of overload, with too much to do and too little time. The RAISE framework, the core of *Focused Fundraising*, took shape with one part mindfulness, one part brain science, one part professional development, and one part organizational optimization. Research and personal interviews verified that distraction and overload threaten cause-related work everywhere. In this book, you will find the common causes of distraction and overload. Once grounded in the realities we all face, you will then learn RAISE—a relevant, practical method to set focused direction for yourself and your team. With a deeper understanding of focus and a new method to practice it, you can help your team climb the Focused Fundraising Maturity ladder.

The constant craziness of nonprofit life is clear to us—not enough resources combined with lots of demands. Many times, more digital tools, data, and choices do not simplify; they complicate. Eventually, we succumb to overload. So, over the past several years we have been asking some big questions of ourselves and our colleagues involved in nonprofit life. Now we turn these questions to you:

- How can you leverage the useful parts of the twenty-first-century work environment while not getting derailed by the distractions?
- How can you meaningfully rely on messages to get work done, and then wade through 300+ emails at the end of the day?
- What do you do if you cannot delegate, or "hold time on your calendar," or otherwise leverage the pithy time management advice we all have heard a thousand times?
- How can you remain responsive to coworkers, kids, and spouses via text without the incessant "dings" distracting you from whatever is in front of you?
- How can you leverage the best digital resources without getting too distracted from the choices and outcomes that matter most?

These questions themselves can be overwhelming. And, when you combine them with personal questions about priorities, the overload can grow even further. How should you organize your time? What priorities must you tackle and what can you ignore? What decisions and actions will yield the best results? What is a waste of time? Some of these questions may affect you. Some of them may affect your entire organization. Are policies and goals clear? Are expectations stated? Are processes efficient? Effective? Neither? What about the tools and systems in place? We promise this book will help you acknowledge the realities and find sustainable ways to rise above the overload.

When we started *Focused Fundraising*, little did we know a global pandemic would amplify the constant craziness. We pledged to not dwell on the pandemic. Most of us will want to forget all or most of 2020 and 2021. For those who could *go to* work, it meant worrying about masks and sanitizer and coughs and community spread. For those who worked from home, it meant Zoom after Teams after BlueJeans after WebEx after Google Hangout and on and on. If you were fortunate enough to escape the serious health and financial implications of COVID-19, you at least suffered from what has seemed like an eternity of Groundhog Days. Try as we did to avoid the pandemic as an overwrought, oversampled, overwhelming situation, one theme reinforced the need for *Focused Fundraising*: **many of us are suffering from a freneticism like no one has experienced in the past.**

Frenetic fundraising feels like the new normal. Frenetic fundraising seems like the only possibility. Even professionals and volunteers who never had trouble with focus began to fray during the pandemic. One fundraising leader known for her Zen-like calm told us that pre-COVID she never looked at her phone in meetings. Since the pandemic, her phone is always out. Zoom fatigue exhausted focus left and right. People who could sit through back-to-back in-person meetings in pre-pandemic days without issue found they tuned out 90 seconds into a virtual meeting. As you will read in the following pages, this is what we are all up against—more email, more texts, more chats, more posts, and more shallow experiences test our ability to stay on purpose and productive. The pandemic has not just damaged focus, it has brought it to a breaking point.

What has been inspiring, though, is that it is possible to gain focus even during a pandemic. We saw a Herculean effort by fundraising operations teams to spin up access, resources, and brand-new processes for work-from-home arrangements. Michael's experiences at Yale were similar to those playing out around the world. We went from "Of course you must handle gift processing in the office" to "Of course we can make it work from home." We went from "When would you like to have lunch to discuss your pledge?" to "Do you prefer Zoom or WebEx to meet up?" As an industry (and a country and a planet), we pivoted and evolved.

How? How did we do things in a matter of days that seemed untenable and impossible just weeks prior? Focus! Well, focus and urgency. Most nonprofits changed the rules of the game in March 2020. It was smart but it was hard. The old saying that "necessity is the mother of all invention" was tested in a massive, real-time experiment. And, it turns out that the saying is true.

With these changes, though, came added distractions. Working from home meant handling kiddos and cats, dogs and doorbells. Attention to detail gets trickier when your office is also your laundry room. Working from the office is not much better. Office time now means coordinating calendars for hoteling spaces, limiting exposures, and prioritizing activities previously handled at the water cooler.

We are all navigating a new landscape. Some technology innovations (especially Zoom, which went from 19 million users in late 2019 to 300 million by December 2020!) irrevocably changed how we work. But change does not mean terrific. The gaps and shortcomings in virtual and hybrid work are apparent. The risks to our work–life balance and focus are clear. It is also clear that we cannot handle the constant craziness of nonprofit life without newfound resilience and a strong sense of purpose. In the following pages, you'll hone your personal style of focus based on a deeper understanding of mindfulness. You'll also learn about causativity, an alternative approach to productivity that incorporates principles of mindfulness.

Focused Fundraising offers you personal and team solutions for the constant craziness. Overcoming overload does not happen overnight. It is a process. What you will find here are stories from professionals and volunteers just like you. Whether you are a volunteer, an operations professional, or on the frontline, you can learn the techniques we provide. You can routinely set focused direction for yourself. You can also regularly set a focused direction for your organization. *Focused Fundraising* can help you make focus a habit.

How to Use This Book

Depending on your interests and goals, you can read *Focused Fundraising* beginning to end, or in a more targeted way. If you are interested in understanding the challenges to focus in nonprofit life, you will want to spend time in Part One, which catalogues the most common sources of distraction and overload based on our research and interviews. As you read it, you may wonder, "Are they talking about me?" If so, take comfort in knowing you are among many, many friends. In all the research we've done, not a single person we've spoken to has said "Overload? Nope, never happens here."

If you want solutions you can try right away, you may want to jump to Part Two, which builds on an understanding of focus from the earlier chapters and gives you a framework called RAISE so you can focus without forcing it. With RAISE, we emphasize the master skill of setting a focused direction. Routinely setting focused direction for yourself means you can fly above distraction and overload. And when you do get bogged down, you can lift your sights back up. How does it work? RAISE was specifically designed for nonprofit fundraising professionals. It builds on the skills of empathy and insight, traits that draw all of us to nonprofit-related work. Each chapter in Part Two elaborates one of the five steps involved in setting focused direction.

If you want to bring greater focus to your team or your organization, you may want to go straight to Part Three, where you may recognize some familiar organizational dynamics that impede focus. However, most importantly, Part Four includes A Focused Fundraising Maturity Model. It was designed based on Chris and his firm's experience consulting top fundraising organizations, combined with Michael's experience with mindfulness, advancement IT, and causativity at Yale. You and your team can use the model to discuss how focused you are today. With candor, you can start anywhere on the model and use it as a backdrop for planning how you can develop greater focus.

If you picked up this book to learn, we hope you take a moment now to reflect on one benefit that would make the read worthwhile.

Is it perhaps less stress? Stretching into a new role? Managing up? If so you may want to really register *instant overload*—the phenomenon of looking at your phone at one message, and getting sucked into five other things. If you're drowning in overwork right now, you may find value in a "round up" exercise called the List, the Mob, and the Waiting Line—a practice you can do any time to create some space for thinking bigger.

No matter where you're starting, we hope *Focused Fundraising* can serve as a stepping-stone for you. We hope it brings focus, joy, and meaning to your nonprofit fundraising work, and helps us all strengthen the work we do to address our collective needs.

PART

I

The Challenges of Focused Fundraising

ARE YOU RUNNING day and night, trying to keep up? Overload is so common, it feels constant. To try to get it all done, we run from meeting to meeting, task to task, always checking for new messages and volleying replies. We are distracted by dozens of things a day that did not exist even a few years ago. To begin to gain focus, we start by recognizing this constant craziness.

1

The Constant Craziness of Nonprofit Life

How ON EDGE are we from the 24/7 nature of nonprofit life?

How real is the constant craziness in nonprofits?

At large universities, hospital systems, internationally focused nonprofits, and small local organizations, we hear edginess from everyone we interview. Consider your daily interactions. What do you hear when you ask a colleague how they are? What do they answer?

Crazy.

Crazy busy.

Crazy has become normal. Flat out. Running. Insane. These are the answers we hear every day.

Crazy can feel good. A pioneer of mindfulness-based stress reduction recognized the thrill of craziness of modern life. Jon Kabat-Zinn used the phrase "full catastrophe living" from *Zorba the Greek* to describe the all-in, all-out nature of a meaningful life. When you are doing important work, you want in on the action. A top annual giving leader we know is like an Energizer® bunny, always revving up her team. A volunteer fundraiser on a small neighborhood youth organization inspires her fellow Board members with her energy every day. This energy fuels meaning, buoyed by cause-related work.

Mindfulness, though, makes the cost of craziness evident. The inspired team leader runs into slower-moving parts of the organization. "Why can't they move faster? Why don't they care? They just don't get it!" Hard-charging volunteers love the action, until they encounter an underresourced staff member just trying to keep the lights on. "Why can't we get going around here?!" We hear the same frustration from individuals trying to get to their priorities. One day they are checking things off the list, feeling good, and the next day the list is 10 times longer. All that running and yet they now feel further behind. These frustrations then intersect with the nonprofit industry's well-documented difficulties with staff retention and pretty soon crazy busy becomes burned out.

Slowing Down Is Not the Answer

The answer to constant craziness is not to slow down. Why would you want to slow down on things that really matter? Your mission deserves and demands urgency. Slowing down is a passion-killer. Slowing down supports the dark-but-sometimes-accurate meme that life is simply repeating "next week things will slow down" every week until you die.

The instinct to slow down is not misplaced, however. Because when busyness slips into overload, burnout is around the corner. Having juggled for too long, we become even more worried that balls will start dropping, and those balls will be the priority ones. If the image of juggling is not anxiety-inducing enough, some nonprofit professionals describe their lives as a house of cards. One bump and it all tumbles. And, of course, there is multi-tasking. Multi-tasking is perhaps the most common dilemma of the modern era. Over time the busyness and multi-tasking leads too many to describe the hassles of nonprofit life—the many irritations of volunteer and team meetings—as "death by a thousand cuts."

Though this may sound bleak, there are alternatives.

In their *Harvard Business Review* article "Stress Can Be a Good Thing If You Know How to Use It," Alia and Thomas Crum draw on their research to explain that acknowledging and understanding stress is essential to avoid being trapped in it. To enjoy work amidst constant craziness is to understand it, and use it. We need to acknowledge mental load.

Thankfully there is growing awareness of mental load. Mental load came to the forefront in 2017 from the feminist cartoon *Emma*. In the cartoon it points out that the majority of a couple or family's mental load often rests with a woman. Who thinks of the medical forms for the kids? Who plans the meals? Who remembers the family commitments? The burden of mental load is not the task itself. It is one thing to take a kid to the doctor because you are asked to do so, it is another thing to schedule the appointment, remember the prep work, get the forms together, write out a list, and ask your spouse to go. Going to the doctor is the task, the planning and remembering is the mental load. And many of us are overloaded by it.

Without acknowledging mental load, the tendency is to strive harder to slow down. Common recommendations are exercise, relaxation, productivity trainings, and so on. All of these can reduce stress and alleviate mental load. However, what if slowing down is not an option you have? What if you do not have the time to exercise? What if sleep does not come easily to you? What if you are a parent, primary caretaker, *and* full-time fundraiser? What if there is a new deadline for a grant proposal that represents 10% of your organization's budget? The mental load from these realities cannot simply be wished away.

To enjoy work amid constant craziness means learning new ways to handle mental load, not necessarily slowing down. What we have discovered in our research and our experience is that there are ways to *think* differently that reduce mental load and uplift energy. Over the past three years we have been conducting interviews, testing techniques, and researching the heavy workload and mental load that affect nonprofit professionals across the country. To share what we have learned from working with wonderful professionals at Yale and hundreds of other nonprofit institutions, we landed on *Focused Fundraising*. Our aim is to help you overcome overload and focus without forcing it.

2

Focus Begins by Valuing the Work

A SOBERING JUNE 7, 2021, *Chronicle of Philanthropy* article on the challenges of retaining top staff stated, "51 percent of fundraisers expected to leave their jobs within two years."

Yes, more than half of fundraising professionals do not expect to stay in their jobs. Why? Time and again, those on the frontlines as well as support staff say they do not feel valued. It is not just professionals who feel that way. Volunteers, who sign up to fundraise, tell us they do not have the support they need. There is a real cost to saying fundraising is important and then acting like it is not. The high rate of turnover and burnout in the nonprofit sector is bordering on a national crisis. Jason Lewis's *The War for Fundraising Talent: And How Small Shops Can Win* provides a stark, one-sentence explanation of the ongoing dynamics: "The [typical] organization lacks the culture to keep [the fundraiser] longer than eighteen months."

Several forces devalue nonprofit fundraising. In a moment, you will read about three demeaning myths that do just that. These three myths disguise fundraising in the popular imagination and belittle it in the eyes of those who do it. The myths add to the hidden mental load, eroding focus. Results are left up to heroic effort by impassioned people working for low or no pay over consistently long periods of time. These purpose-defeating myths lead some of the best in the field to pack up their bags and go. And when they go, the causes they support suffer.

Myth #1: Fundraising Is Primarily About Money

I could never do THAT—I hate to ask people for money.

If you are in fundraising, have you ever heard this? And, if you are not in fundraising, have you ever said it? This is the basis for Eloise Brice's *Don't Make Me Fundraise*. If you are dipping your toes into fundraising, have you thought it or felt it? If you are a volunteer and you have been asked to fundraise, has this been rattling around in your head?

To hate asking people for money is to be human. Asking for money is associated with begging. But why continue to frame fundraising in this way? Most everyone is okay with recommending that a friend pay to eat at a certain restaurant or buy a certain app. So, what is so different about recommending that a friend donate to a nonprofit organization? We offer such consumer and personal recommendations daily to our friends and colleagues, yet that helpfulness can feel icky when philanthropy is involved. The misperception about asking people for money persists, despite the fact that we have never met a professional or a seasoned volunteer who viewed their fundraising work as primarily about asking people for money. Is money a part of the process? Yes. Is money the sole purpose of it? No.

Part of the reason fundraising is not well understood is that it is not generally taught as a discipline until graduate school. Did you choose fundraising, development, or advancement in college? High school? After a different career? The nonprofit sector represents 10% of the U.S. gross domestic product (GDP), yet most Americans are scarcely aware of the profession funding these nonprofits.

People get into nonprofit fundraising because they fall into it. For focused fundraisers, the reason they stick with it despite common misperceptions is because it is primarily *not* about soulless transactions. Many other jobs may be about money, but excelling in the field of fundraising means shifting your frame. Fundraising is a blend of meaning and money. Money, yes—because money is necessary. But not because money is the primary concern. Fundraising is first about relationships, purpose, and supporting a cause through goodwill and donations, not the financial transactions themselves.

Focused Fundraising puts focus first. Focus relies on a strong sense of purpose. In very tangible ways, nonprofit professionals and seasoned volunteers demonstrate purpose. They donate to the organizations they invite others to donate to. They recommend donating because they have a personal relationship with the cause. They lead by example. In this book you will meet focused fundraising teams who do exactly this, even in extremely trying circumstances.

Myth #2: Fundraising Is Brainless Cheerleading

Try a quick experiment. Close your eyes for 30 seconds and imagine someone who is a great fundraiser. Picture the qualities of this person. What do they look like? What is their personality like? How do they sound to you?

Cheerful. Upbeat. Peppy. Enthusiastic. Or, for those with a negative view on fundraising, aggressive, pushy, in-your-face. Too often we hear the negative descriptions. Of course, these more negative qualities might be involved in fundraising, but they are not the most important parts, as any seasoned professional or volunteer will tell you.

Fundraising for nonprofits does not fit generic stereotypes. Quite simply, many people view it as "Sales, but for a good cause." There may be some truth to that statement, but not a lot. The pushiest used car salesman imaginable may come to mind. "What can I do to get you in this baby today?" If one's view is not of the pushy salesman, then the image is often of the cheer squad. Bake sales. Car washes. Gala events. All of these viewpoints may have some real-world application, but not a lot. In too many cases, the fundraiser is seen as someone who can be brainlessly cheerful, hold out a bucket, and just collect the change being tossed in.

Focused fundraising has nothing to do with this myth. Focused fundraising means recognizing a basic and important fact about fundraising. It is a fact so essential to long-term success in fundraising, it often goes unspoken. Those we most admire in the profession know it well. The focused fundraisers you will meet in this book, whether they are at elite universities or small churches, know it. And if you have had more than a few years of experience in some facet of fundraising, you know it. Quite simply, it is this: *Focused fundraising is thought work.*

Fundraising is thought work. Cultivation, solicitation, and stewardship all require strategy, planning, coordination, discipline, and a high degree of emotional intelligence. Expert practitioners do not view fundraising principally as "the ask," because they know how much emotional and thought work goes into creating the conditions for success at the moment of the ask. Why does the organization need funds in the first place? Why do people and organizations support it? Why does a particular person support it? How will they know their support is being put to good purposes? And so on. To paraphrase veteran fundraising coach Chuck Loring, "A well-staged solicitation is like the cashier asking if you want to use debit or credit." The thought work was all of the cultivation to get to a well-orchestrated Yes. The real big-picture thinking on the whole process is like the advertising for the store, the layout of the aisles, the messaging and branding throughout, and the engagement of the staff with the customer. The checkout is simply one part of that process.

It has been our privilege to put this book together after spending time with professionals of all stripes at some of the best fundraising organizations in the world. What we have found is that the best of the best are *thought workers* first and foremost. They connect with *why* their organization needs support and they align it with people who also connect to the cause and want to make a difference. You will hear some of their stories and learn some of their focus and organizational techniques in this book. Most importantly, if you understand fundraising as thought work, you will see why focus is so crucial to results.

Myth #3: Fundraising Is Done by a Solo Solicitor

Nothing strikes fear into the heart of novices quite like the ask. What if the person says no?

A real ask is based on a real relationship. Donations of any size are usually the culmination of intentional relationship-building and, in some cases, extensive negotiations. The moment of solicitation is critical, of course, but it is part of a relationship, and that relationship usually involves many people and many processes. While this is especially true for a large donation, focused fundraisers know that "large" should be in the eye of the donor, not a number they think is big.

Debunking this myth is important because it applies to everyone who works with or around individual fundraisers but do not make the ask. You yourself may not be a solo solicitor. You might be an administrator or faculty member, direct mail marketer, event organizer, gift processor, IT professional, stewardship writer, finance professional, volunteer, or any one of dozens of positions that fundraising depends on. Because fundraising is thought work, it requires a team of dedicated thought workers, all of whom care about the organization and the mission it serves.

Moving from "I am not a solicitor" to "We are a fundraising team, and I can help" improves team results. Why are *we* raising money? Whom do these funds serve? How does giving serve the donor? Why do people want to give to us? These deceptively simple questions are best answered not just by one or a few people who are involved in direct solicitations of donors, but by the whole team that is involved in supporting the organization. Hopefully this includes everyone. Why? Why must everyone know? Why must everyone care?

Focused fundraising is a team effort. The unique aspect of nonprofit enterprise is that a financial surplus does not go to any individual. It goes to advance the purpose of the organization. To maximize results, everyone needs to be in. Everyone needs to join in the thought work. Everyone needs to focus. Seeing it as a team effort further highlights the importance of focus, individually and collectively.

Value Leads to More Value

When these three myths are debunked, a heavy load gets lighter.

Top fundraisers and volunteers do not limit themselves by these three myths. They do not accept the unspoken misperceptions that non-fundraisers often have. They know fundraising's worth. And they enroll others in valuing fundraising and helping to get it the support it needs.

Valuing the work is a critical first step for focus. The next step is to understand the many obstacles that interfere with focus. Often valuing the work is crowded out by daily dings and pings. The average nonprofit professional might receive 20+ emails an hour. While editing one afternoon, Michael received a text with a sad emoji and the number "502." It was a text from one of the fundraising leaders at Yale, and 502 was the number of unread emails in her inbox.

To develop focus amidst the constant craziness, we need to walk down a tricky road together, a road to understanding overload and distraction. We say tricky because it requires some introspection and some reflective thinking. If you can make the time to read and reflect, you will begin to recognize focus without forcing it. This will help you apply RAISE—an indispensable tool to elevate focus.

3

You Can Focus Because You Are Mindful

WHAT HAPPENS WHEN chaos and mindfulness meet? They become friends.

We met in 2015. It did not take long to realize that ours would be a yin and yang relationship. Chris has been described as Captain Chaos. Michael has been called Mr. Mindfulness. Chris may have spent as much time in the filtered air of airplanes as Michael has spent in the quiet air of silent meditation. And yet, at the core, we have a similar set of values. We are both married with two children roughly the same age. We are both driven by quality of life, including quality time with our families and friends. And we both want to use our time on the planet to address needs that affect us all.

Yale hired Chris and his colleagues at Zuri Group to advise and consult Michael and team on an advancement technology turnaround project. Yale had introduced a new CRM in 2012 and, as of 2015, it was not going well. Michael was put in charge of the project to reimplement the system. Happily, as a result of the project, there was a dramatic turnaround in the attitudes of Yale's team members toward the CRM and how it supported their work. In this process, Michael learned how to handle the chaos of an enormously complex project, and Chris learned how to be more mindful each step of the way. During our CRM project at Yale, we saw the advantage of mindfulness in action. We inquired more deeply into the challenges team members were having. We stopped telling people what they needed. We listened and asked more questions. The project was not perfect, and it was a humbling experience. It taught us an important lesson about distraction and focus. One of Michael's mentors, David Allen, who wrote the best seller *Getting Things Done*, likes to say, "the mind is for having ideas, not holding them." What to do with all the goals, ideas, thoughts, plans, issues? What we learned is that mindfulness is the ultimate aid to focus.

Mindfulness Aids Focus

Mindfulness aids focus? Doesn't mindfulness slow things down? Isn't mindfulness about taking a breather? Who has time to be mindful?

Mindfulness can, of course, hinder progress. If you see it as "stopping to smell the roses," then sure, anyone can stop responding to do just one or two things. But of course that has negative consequences. So, based on this misperception that it's about stopping, mindfulness remains aspirational—like a good idea for when there's time to savor the moment. It's hard to find the time for mindfulness if it's about stopping. So, while you might be thinking "I need to be mindful," a notification pops up, and then three more. It seems impossible to believe that you could both keep up progress and also be mindful.

Mindfulness is misunderstood strictly as slowing down to smell the roses. Slowing down can be one of the most self-defeating things you can do. As Zen philosopher Alan Watts points out, it can be like "beating a drum in search of a fugitive." Although there may be practices to help you slow down and "quiet the mind," it is too simplistic to boil down mindfulness—a recently coined term—from the rich and varied traditions involving eons of emotional, spiritual, and human development all over the world.

How we use the word mindfulness in *Focused Fundraising* is based on years of practice, personal experience, reading, and interviews with leaders in meditation and emotional intelligence. In *The Mind*

Illuminated, neuroscientist and lifelong meditation practitioner John Yates says this about mindfulness:

"Mindfulness" is a somewhat unfortunate translation of the Pali word *sati* because it suggests being attentive, or remembering to pay attention. This doesn't really capture the full meaning and importance of *sati*. Even without *sati*, we're *always* paying attention to *something*. But with *sati* we pay attention to the right things, and in a more skillful way.

A wise mentor at Yale, Meredith Fahey, pointed out that in order to take a deep dive you need to leap from higher up. We incorporate techniques from mindfulness traditions throughout this book. As you read, there will be no way to avoid honest self-appraisal, which can be humbling. However, we believe that you have an advantage if you chose the constant craziness of nonprofit life. If you made that choice, you know how to put something ahead of yourself. We believe that the ability to put a cause first, whether that is an organizational mission, a CRM system, or a family member's needs, is the platform for focus. Mindfulness does not slow things down; it strengthens purpose.

Mindfulness is primarily about nonjudgmental honesty—genuine recognition of what is going on. It is not about going faster or slower per se, just about noticing without judgment. And when you start to notice your own heart and mind, you cannot help but notice the spin.

Spinning Forward

Throughout *Focused Fundraising* we use the metaphor of spinning. A spinning mind is a normal mind. The question we pose to you as you reflect on focus, is how do you spin *forward*? How do you consistently spin in a focused direction?

A buzzing, spinning mind is a feature of modern life because there is so much to do. Rather than spinning in place or spinning out of control, spinning forward is how we can work with our active minds and point them in a direction. We believe everyone wants their wheels spinning in some direction. And for a team, it works best when everyone's wheels are spinning in the same direction. Of course, directing the spin is an art. As workers in a sector that is about doing good, our best direction starts from the inside and moves out, as Alan Fine, best selling author and inventor of "InsideOut" coaching, puts it. "Inside" means considering core well-being, especially yours. In fundraising, this can be a good reminder to start with your purpose, your key stakeholders, and your values when spinning up your plans.

We spin because we care. And, because we care, there is chaos. Never in human history has there been such an opportunity and challenge to focus. The good news is that anyone can *choose* to spin rather than be spun. It is a matter of tapping into what you care about and using it to set direction. When you focus in this manner you realize what Tim Gallwey, author of the *Inner Game* series, calls "the art of relaxed concentration." In the next chapter you will begin to connect mindfulness with common distractions.

4

The Tech Tug and Instant Overload

In some ways, technology is like a tug boat. It can help guide your movement in a highly productive way. It can also drag you around in circles.
—Tim Stringer, founder, Technically Simple

ONE OF THE biggest challenges to focus is the tech tug, which is the incessant pull of devices and data. Our devices, our data, our tech, are always seeking our attention. New message? New notification? New update?

The gravitational-like force of the tech tug affects focus at multiple levels. In this chapter we look first at how the tech tug affects organizations. How does your organization view new tech? Is it drawn in every direction by new shiny objects? Is it intentional about the evaluation and selection of new tech? Will new tech solve all its problems? The organizational tech tug is as pervasive as the tug of your phone when you first wake up in the morning.

The personal tech tug is familiar to all of us. This is the day-to-day pull of dings and pings via messages, meetings, media, and management, also known as the 4 Ms, which we will describe further in the following chapters.

Once you have a good handle on the personal tech tug, it becomes easier to recognize instant overload, a common cause of distraction. Having a good handle on the tech tug, instant overload, and distraction gives you a stronger foundation for focus.

The Organizational Tech Tug: Keeping Up with the Dot-Joneses

Whether you entered nonprofit life in the 1960s, 2000s, or last year, you are bound up in a quintessentially American, and rapidly evolving, sector. Peter Drucker, the great management thinker of the twentieth century, considered the "third sector"—nonprofits—the most novel instrument of a free society. Drucker was presaged by de

Tocqueville who, roughly a hundred years earlier, observed the importance of associations to American life. The nonprofit is essential to American life. However, it is in danger. Today's nonprofits and nonprofit professionals are challenged every day to keep up with the pace and demands of technological change.

To fundraise today, you need better apps, more data, more virtual tech, more viral posts, better reporting, and more insights. The world tugs at you and your organization for better, faster data, tech, and digital. Forget the Rolodex and shaking hands at big events, you need the Ice Bucket Challenge. "Giving Days" supplant calendared annual fund asks. Social media replaces coffee-table glossy magazines.

The tech tug pulls individuals and organizations in a thousand directions. Email campaigns, content creation, social media, virtual events, and texting often just fuel the constant craziness. The call for nonprofits and fundraising to keep up does not come from one voice or one new piece of tech. It is not the iPhone or texting that is calling for change. What is calling for change are the expectations of people whom you want to become donors. We, as people, are being conditioned. The gamification of our brains has never been more effectively Pavlovian. Competing for attention has become the most essential skill in for-profit enterprise. Mining data is the primary engine for growth among the new economy's leaders. In the fundraising space, we compete with Facebook, Amazon, and Google for clicks. Tech is about immediacy. Real-time data and decisions turn a 12-month direct mail calendar into a dinosaur.

Blindly following the organizational tech tug only feeds the constant craziness. Consumer expectations are set by trillion-dollar companies, which make nonprofit employees and constituents feel relative deprivation. Tools and resources in the nonprofit sector do not compare.

Nonprofits do not have the resources of the dot-Joneses. Experimentation is not bad, but chasing shiny objects means real objects and real people do not get what they need. For years Chris has been calling this "the iPhone problem" and explaining how it is damaging the nonprofit sector.

The Organizational Tech Tug Means Continuous Change Management

Fundraising pros and seasoned volunteers recognize that blindly giving in to the organizational tech tug does not work. Neither does blindly following the for-profit sector.

Generally, the nonprofit space tends to lag behind for-profit entities in terms of strategy, plans, operations, and resources, not to mention technology infrastructure and data architecture. In for-profit enterprise, entire business models and industries are being rethought based on disruptions in technology (e.g., value chain, digital currencies, and subscription revenue models). For-profit enterprises use social listening techniques, evangelists, and influencers to borrow from traditional fundraising techniques that are all enabled by sophisticated digital toolkits. Nonprofits can learn from this and adapt, too. Not blindly, though.

Consider how nonprofits evaluate fundraising portfolios. Have a look at "machine learning" scores, decipher what they mean, try to factor in context that the model might not (such as, "Jane just told me she is getting a divorce but I do not think that is accommodated in the predictive analytics"), and then make a choice. Keep the prospect? Reassign? What coding is needed? Is there a more effective strategy? Does the prospect warrant another discussion? The technology is better, but nonprofits and individuals must still explain the models and adapt to the insights. We delve into this critical set of work in Chapter 14.

The dilemma of continuous change is ancient. A review of Harari's *Sapiens: A Brief History of Humankind* presents the gripping reality our forebears faced. Millennia ago, Sapiens won out over Neanderthals because Neanderthals "could [not] adapt their social behavior to rapidly changing challenges." In today's organizations the tech tug means learning how to make decisions more quickly.

As Klingberg's *The Overflowing Brain* reminds us, we are working with pretty old hardware. Our brains are not bigger than they were millennia ago, yet we do seem to have to process more data and deal with more choice and noise. So better and better tech is needed to cut through the noise—but it also creates more. What to do? As we get further into *Focused Fundraising*, we will return to the importance of change management.

The Personal Tech Tug

On a personal level, the tech tug is the incessant pings and dings of devices and wearables, which we refer to as the 4 Ms. These are the messages, meetings, media, and management minutiae, like disruptive notifications, that feed the constant craziness. Our phones or wearable tech itself are not the issue. It is that all of us have access to more people, tools, data, and information than we could possibly imagine. In the name of always being connected, we are always reachable. Our sense of boundaries between nonprofit life and home life are constantly under fire.

We are immersed in a digital environment. We move in and out of it with little awareness. In fact, we are rarely aware of how immersive it is until we are someplace without Wi-Fi or cell service. Diving into this book may give you a different picture of devices and your connection to them, and it may bring some of your habits into stark relief. Ideally, in the process of tackling those tendencies, you can uncover other areas where your focus—your "why"—gets lost in the shuffle of your multi-tasking days.

One of the clearest and scariest aspects of the tech tug is its reflexive quality. As we go a bit further into focus and the brain, it is important to know that the tech tug keeps us in a reflexive brain state, meaning we are just waiting to react to the next thing like a pinball. This can obscure our real needs. In *Brainchains* by Theo Compenolle, a treasure trove of ideas and insights, he explains that a "tired manual worker can still fix 100 bolts an hour because most of the routine manual work is taken over by his tireless reflex brain .... However, working harder and longer will not improve the quantity and quality of your brainwork, but make it worse." The tech tug means it is easier to reply than to think. We can all be pinball workers and volley dozens of messages with prebuilt responses, but when the day ends, we have no idea what we said or did.

Despite the reflexive power of it, the tech tug itself is not necessarily bad. Yes, it can be difficult to decompress. Yes, it can mean screen fatigue. But what really makes it a problem is that it leads to distraction. In order to understand this in a mindful way, it is important to understand instant overload. On the surface it is easy to think that the dings and pings themselves are the distraction. But if you dig into it further you see the options and opportunities that mindfulness presents. There is always choice present, but first you need to recognize the ever-present power of instant overload.

Instant Overload

The tech tug is unceasing. Our phones beckon "check me!" at all hours and in all places, no matter how unseemly.

Then, instant overload takes hold.

It takes mindfulness to spot instant overload. To spot it in action, let's consider an example.

Imagine you are in a meeting on Zoom and that you are kind of bored. Someone is talking about an issue you have talked about several times. Still, you are trying to be courteous and listen. Then you feel a vibration in your pocket from your phone. First you were trying to listen and now there is a buzz from your phone. With the buzzing, you are in a bit of bind, right? You feel the urge to check your phone. It is killing you to not know what that the vibration meant. It could be anyone. Anything. On the other hand, you know it would be rude to your meeting mates to check your phone. So, what do you do? Do you follow the vibration in your pocket, or follow the vibe in the Zoom room? This is the tech tug at work, and now you are in instant overload.

Instant overload is where choice hides. So, before we slap the label "distraction" on following the vibration from your phone, we need to acknowledge that there is a moment of choice. You can choose to stick with the person talking to you (boring) or the unknown cause of your phone's vibration (interesting). If you choose to stick with your meeting mate, but you are thinking about what the vibration might mean, you are distracted. If you glance at your watch and ignore the person talking to you, you are distracted. What are you to do? That is instant overload. This highlights our love/hate relationship with tech: we love and want these cool tools and they can help, but they can and often do diminish focus.

Throughout *Focused Fundraising* we talk about elevating focus, not forcing it. The tech tug is a great way to practice because we face it countless times every day. If you follow your phone's vibration, you are likely distracted. If you ignore it but think about it, you are likely distracted. This is a "damned if you do, damned if you don't" situation. It is the essence of instant overload.

Instant overload can drive distraction, but it doesn't have to. You have a choice. Your choice can be to focus, not by forcing yourself (which is just another distraction), but by understanding yourself and your tendencies to focus. If you blindly follow the tech tug, you'll be in it nonstop. As productivity guru Tim Stringer says, "If you say 'yes' to every app that wants to notify you, you're welcoming instant overload."

Every day, nonprofit professionals and volunteers are subject to the same tech tugs as our for-profit colleagues at Google and Apple. Each day, we run out of time and often end the workday without having accomplished the most meaningful work due to the most persistent minutiae. As Cal Newport's *Deep Work* suggests, we then too often return to a "second shift" late at night to try to keep up. It is a never-ending loop. Survey after survey shows that it is a struggle to keep up. As a result, our best bet is to learn. We can get curious. We can engage mindfulness and make choices. How *do* we direct our attention? In short, we can elevate focus. To do so we need to reckon with the 4 Ms.

5

Why Instant Overload Is Here to Stay: The 4 Ms

*We do not rise to the level of our expectations; we fall to
the level of our training.*

—Archilocus, Greek poet

INSTANT OVERLOAD IS the price of needing to know. We want to know what everything means. We want to know everything that's going on. Every ping and ding has potential meaning. FOMO strikes if the latest text goes unread. Sadly, all this information blocks the very meaning we seek by overloading our minds. Perhaps no one expresses the reality of overload better than Daniel J. Levitin in *The Organized Mind*. He writes:

In 2011, Americans took in five times as much information every day as they did in 1986—the equivalent of 175 newspapers. During our leisure time, not counting work, each of us processes 34 gigabytes or 100,000 words every day.

Today these figures may well have doubled. For context, this book is 60,000 words—well shy of a typical day's worth of information.

There is no way around it. There is so much on our minds. There has to be. And when we dip into our phone to check our inboxes, and we spot three other messages, and then follow a link ... overload is right there. Yet, it's necessary to know what's going on. Part of our work in fundraising is to listen to "signals from the modern donor," as Cooper and Bailey describe in their book *Responsive Fundraising*. The next message or mention could be just that one that either convinces a donor to click "donate now" or pushes us into instant overload.

As you will see, rising above overload is not a matter of trying harder or forcing yourself. It is about gaining a stronger understanding of the challenges to focus. So now we turn to the most common and vexing contributors, the 4 Ms: messages, meetings, media, and management.

Messages. For the nonprofit professionals and volunteers we interviewed and surveyed, email messages can be particularly overwhelming. Even "zero inbox" practitioners like Travis Soyer and David Nolan at Texas Christian University, interviewed later in the book, indicated difficulty with sticking with the practice. This is an oldie but a goodie. If we piled on Slack, Teams, Chatter, and other instant messaging work tools here, you can see where instant overload creeps in countless times a day. Chris, for instance, maintains Teams accounts with around 10 clients in addition to his 65-person team, leading to a remarkable volume of pings and dings during the day. Silencing these only results in overwhelming mounds of messages to wade through at the end of the day. With each ping, you might wonder: "What does that mean? What to do?"

Meetings. In our surveying and interviews, we heard repeatedly that meetings often represented "time sucks" for participants. The move to Zoom appears to have increased the number of meetings. There seems to be some evidence that video conference call benefits, such as remaining in one place, removing physical barriers like room size as a factor, and others, have improved participants' experiences. For every beneficiary of virtual meetings, though, there is likely some extrovert dying just a little bit. The tech tug and instant overload have never been more powerful than in virtual meetings. How can you resist multi-tasking? It seems no one can, which we will return to later.

Media, namely written and video content delivered via our smartphones and on tantalizing and engaging apps such as Facebook, LinkedIn, Instagram, TikTok, and others, can make the time lost in meetings seem like a tea party compared to the hours wasted online. Here is a quick and risky exercise (because you might get so distracted you will not return to the book): go to your iPhone, open the "Settings," then "Screen Time." How many hours did you average this week? For Chris, the total is routinely over eight hours ... per day! His iPhone is his daily phone for work, but phone time is not the primary culprit. Email, followed by Safari (for all of his daily papers and articles), then messages, followed by LinkedIn and Facebook take his attention. On average, he picks up his phone 86 times a day (yep, that is a statistic the iPhone tracks). Ironically, the iPhone does not seem to track how many minutes per day Chris is actually on phone calls, a metric that has decreased since video conferencing has expanded but still requires a few hours a day.

Management distractions are multifold. They take two main forms: managers and metrics. Those responsible for our day-to-day and overall planning (managers) are sometimes to blame for the whiplash and overload we feel. It is also common that the lack of strategic planning and shared protocols leads to confusion, which leads to inefficiency due to a lack of focus. Ironically, even well-intentioned directives can result in distractions that diminish outcomes. And, the minutiae that management sometimes adds to the equation of our day—aka TPS Reports from the movie Office Space—can take a real toll. Metrics are similarly suspect in delivering value. Well-designed metrics certainly add focus, yet too often the number, clarity, and time-to-create aspects of metrics arrangements do not deliver on their promise of better behavior. In both the person-based and metric-based senses of management, many professionals can get less utility from these arrangements than the costs imposed.

Phronetic Leadership and Managing Management

The idea of "phronesis," translated as practical wisdom or good judgment, is as old as books about focus. Since the Greeks initiated most of the philosophical principles we continue to espouse, Aristotle and others have presented the notion that virtues of character ground ethical decision-making; leaders who demonstrate practical wisdom are able to consistently sort through seemingly endless variables in complex scenarios to consistently arrive at an ethical decision (e.g., decisions that are pragmatic, realistically achievable, and made in the interest of the common good). This decision-making process can be summarized as seeking the "golden mean," or middle ground. Plato had his philosopher kings; these days, Hawken Brackett, the executive director of strategic engagement at the University of Alabama, recommends that we favor practical wisdom over "technical rationality" in order to be better managers and leaders. Brackett wrote his dissertation on the topic and explained to Chris how it can be useful to fundraisers. The idea that fundraising should heavily rely on ethics and virtues of character is clear. The corollary idea—that metrics and "technically rational" measures are overly prescriptive—isolates the challenge in fundraising. We must not prioritize efficiency at the cost of being effective. While we must be targeted and data-driven to guide our micro and macro decisions, we also need to put donors (and our focus on them) first, which may not align with the numbers. When in doubt, Brackett suggests leaders should default to their virtues.

Should We Expect More or Less Distraction?

You get the sense of how the 4 Ms can fuel the constant craziness. You can also likely see how we are destined for more distraction in the future.

Moore's Law states that computer-processing capacity doubles around every two years. Cloud software company Domo sees the growth of data storage in the cloud as exponential; they predict that by 2025, the 2.5 quintillion bytes of data created each day will aggregate into over 200 zettabytes in cloud storage. To understand what this meant, we had to look it up. A zettabyte is 1 followed by 21 zeroes; that is, a trillion gigabytes, equivalent to the storage in billions of iPhones. It's staggering to consider how much new data and tech is being produced and how its tug will likely continue to grow. As Paulos's work in Chapter 9 shows, we humans have a hard time with huge numbers. And, we just learned from Levitin's *Organized Mind* that we are processing at least five times more information than we were in the past millennia. What does this mean? We are inundated with content and complications, making it easy for the urgent to overwhelm the meaningful.

It is also important to consider demographic trends. As donors live longer and remain active with our institutions into their later years, we should expect more contact with them and their families. In his book *2030*, Mauro Guillén argues persuasively for the growing Gray Market, aka the purchasing power of senior citizens. On a numerically smaller but important level, this leads to growth in our databases. That is, donors living an extra, say, 10 years will lead to measurable growth in the data we manage. Understanding this growth may come from new applications of machine learning and artificial intelligence. All signs point to more data and therefore more potential for distraction and overload, unless you and your team develop strategies to cope with these dynamics.

Can Our Amazing Brains Cope with the 4 Ms?

The literature on how we learn, how we focus, and, well, how the brain works is as voluminous as it is complicated. We highly recommend starting with Harari's *Sapiens*, Klingberg's *The Overflowing Brain*, and the relevant works of the Heath brothers, Levitt, and Gladwell. Their books are referenced throughout *Focused Fundraising*.

It is amazing how the brain works. Have you ever noticed that when you are in a movie theater you might not always notice how the people right in front of you get up and leave but you do see them return out of the corner of your eye?

To deal with change and large volumes of information, our amazing brains default to what is called preattentive processing. In that movie theater, preattentive processing is your brain protecting you. For millennia, our brains have been trained to notice things as they come into view to assess the potential threat of that newly spotted thing. However, when someone who has been seated 20 feet in front of you for an hour stands up in a dark theater to go get more popcorn, you may not notice them leaving at all. This is how our brain is designed to focus. It is pretty amazing.

This sort of preattentive processing plays a role in most of the ways we deal with the 4 Ms. For all time, humans have noticed that fire is hot and faster predators with teeth might eat you. To survive and thrive, our senses adapted. Our eyes and ears seek out those abnormal, external signs for clues. These days, tigers are not as much a risk as going down a rabbit hole on Reddit. **Bolded text** is different than the rest and gets our attention. A flashing icon on our phone catches our eye. When you read this next statement—"your phone dings as a text is received"—your brain is likely actually replaying the exact sound you have heard and become all too familiar with. "Diinnggg!" just rang through your head as a result of how the brain works. This tendency is central to how we get distracted. You might have even looked at or touched your phone. You are hooked! Media and messages, not to mention meetings, metrics, and other managerial minutiae, overload and distract you at every turn.

Our brains are trying to understand the many, many stimuli at any given moment. All of those emails, all of those text messages, all of those other digital interruptions represent activity that our brain needs to understand. And we are not exactly built for this. The volume of interaction, the volume of interruption, and the importance of these interruptions are challenging to discern. In fact, for a terrific explanation on this subject, read Torkel Klingberg's *The Overflowing Brain: Information Overload and the Limits of Working Memory*. Despite our brains staying almost the same size and shape for 40,000-plus years, human brains now must process exponentially more information than in the past.

We Are All in It Together

In 2020, in preparation for this book and before the pandemic hit, we interviewed and polled fundraising professionals to get some insights on the overload and distraction we all face. If 2020 poll responses are a good indicator, nonprofit professionals should expect that email and meetings will top their list of distractions, followed closely by poor reporting and analysis options.

It is the volume of distractions and frequency of noise that makes focused fundraising so challenging to attain. It has gotten worse. Collectively, we are likely more distracted than we were before the pandemic. A 2020 survey of 80 fundraising professionals across the United States demonstrates these trends. For starters, this group of mostly fundraising executives and directors found that 92% experienced "information overload." All the distractions—the 4 Ms—have made 67% feel like it has gotten worse in the past five years, as depicted in Figure 5.1.

The sources of distraction and overload are important to understand. In this survey, reporting, data, and technology were top culprits for respondents. Of course, for frontline fundraisers, it is

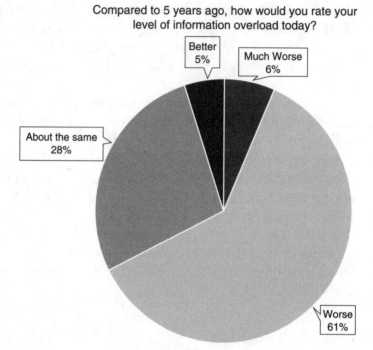

Compared to 5 years ago, how would you rate your
level of information overload today?

Better
5%

Much Worse
6%

About the same
28%

Worse
61%

Figure 5.1   How Overloaded Are We?

likely that their day-to-day roles—engaging and soliciting donors—
can feel overwhelming. Beyond most of the respondent's day-
to-day work, though, there are many areas that result in serious
distractions. Figure 5.2 presents that stark reality for many
fundraising professionals.

While the data depict the challenges faced on average, it is specific
cases and examples that often prove the point most clearly. Looking at
a typical day in the life of a fellow fundraiser sheds light on the other
choices and distractions that can lead us astray.

A Day in the Life

Check your phone first thing in the morning?
    Check in meetings?
    Check while waiting?
    And every time you check, respond now or later?

This is the vexing conundrum of the tech tug and instant overload. It is especially so for those who focus on major, principal, and planned giving: you never know which message might be one that matters.

Picture this: Steve, an academic fundraising leader, is meeting with a consultant. They are planning how to grow the team. Team growth is Steve's number-one priority for the year. The discussion is deep and fruitful. They are analyzing comparative data and benchmarks to make the case to the dean. While in intense conversation, Steve's phone rings.

Respond now or later?

This situation did happen. Chris was the consultant. Steve did not recognize the caller's number and did not know whether it would be important, but his general policy was: respond. And in this case it paid off. On the other end of the line was an attorney for a prospective donor with a tax problem. That donor had a fast-approaching quarterly tax filing and wanted to make a generous gift immediately.

Spontaneous wins are a fickle friend. That call, that email, that text, that meeting ... all of these are urgent often before we know if they are important. One win amidst dozens of distractions keeps the dopamine flowing.

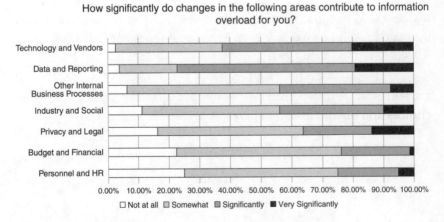

Figure 5.2 What Contributes to Information Overload?

How to Focus with the Four Ms?

According to Alan Fine, coauthor of the best-selling *You Already Know How to Be Great*, your biggest opportunities lie in applying what you know. Applying what you know is harder than ever. Since information is so abundant, choosing what to apply is exceedingly difficult. The best place to start is understanding focus more deeply.

No one knows how to handle your workload and mental load better than you. Typical pop-psych methods to deal with the 4 Ms rely on alpha logic. Alpha logic is thinking that if we study top performers and see what they do, and then apply their tactics to ourselves, we will also raise our level. This strategy rarely works because it leads people to force themselves into habits they cannot sustain (e.g., zero inbox, no-meeting Fridays, and so on). An alternative to alpha logic is genuine self-reflection. Mindfulness. Rather than following best practices, identify practices that work best for you and then improve them sustainably. It is an approach we will be advocating for throughout *Focused Fundraising*.

The tech tug and instant overload can derail even the most focused teams and individuals. The potential for overload and distraction has never been higher. The 4 Ms help us see how ripe our daily life is for distraction, yet there are strategies to overcome overload. Before we introduce you to the RAISE method for setting focused direction, we must first show what we mean by focus without forcing it. Otherwise, focusing will continue to be a battle waged inside yourself. Rather, with *Focused Fundraising* we want you to use the mindfulness and care that you have for causes you support to focus more naturally and easily. This is where we turn next.

6

This Is Not the Focus You're Looking For

What gets us into trouble is not what we do not know.
It is what we know for sure that just ain't so.

—Mark Twain

In *The Art of Gathering*, Priya Parker reminds us that "people are often elsewhere." Lost in our phones. Lost in thought. Down a rabbit hole. All of us have a lot going on. Focus begins with self-awareness.

However, self-awareness is not self-criticism. Conventional advice on focus rarely sticks and rarely reduces overload. Zero-inbox techniques will not prevent messages from being oversent and underthought. Blocked calendar techniques will not prevent meetings from being overscheduled and underplanned. Apps and planners will not prevent digital media from overinforming and underdistilling. And no management technique will prevent nonprofit professionals from too often being overworked and underpaid. Most tactics tackle some of the symptoms but not the root causes.

Focused Fundraising will not give you the same old guidance. There are mountains of books with strategies to enhance focus. But how many of them give you a good understanding of what focus is and is not? You are likely well aware of the benefits of sleep, exercise, nutrition, eliminating distractions, taking breaks, spending time in nature, and other ways to enhance focus. This guidance is valuable, of course, yet it is difficult to apply, mostly because it does not clarify focus in personally relevant ways. So, we present an understanding of focus to clear up some common misperceptions. From this understanding, you and your colleagues can spot the tech tug and instant overload more easily. You can cut down on spinning your wheels. Based on our experience, a clearer understanding of focus (what it is and is not) leads to greater energy even if you do not block your calendar or move to a zero inbox. It is like shifting to a higher elevation. That's how you focus without forcing it.

Maggie's Story

If you interview a top fundraiser, they will tell you how important focus is. They will also tell you that it is not easy to sustain.

One of the top fundraisers at Yale (we will call her Maggie) illustrates how an understanding of focus can evolve. Maggie is a model focused fundraiser. She has a strong sense of mission and purpose. She is intrinsically motivated. She wants to excel and make a difference. She puts the interests of the organization and donors ahead of her own. She looks at opportunities from a win-win perspective. Year after year she conjures up gift opportunities others miss. Researchers, report writers, analysts, and support staff are inspired by her.

Recently, Maggie came to talk with Michael about what she could stop doing in order to focus on what really matters. She was not seeing a lot of room to let anything go to help her reach the next level of performance. She had attended one of Michael's workshops, and she was curious what she could do to make more room for the big, complex opportunities that she was after.

Choosing a Focus

Before we return to Maggie's story to see what she realized, we need to unpack focus. There is no one-size-fits-all definition. We want you to have a personally relevant one.

There are countless definitions of focus by productivity experts, psychologists, and mindfulness gurus. Although Webster's dictionary defines focus as "directed attention," that somehow does not capture the essence of what it's like to *be* focused. We want you to clarify the kind of focus you have in mind as you read this book. You will see in this chapter that there is quite a bit of nuance. Maggie, when she approached Michael for tips or ideas, was voicing a question like: "How do I make space for consistently high performance?" She was looking to engage a particular kind of focus. Is this a question you are asking? Or are you asking different questions?

Take a moment and consider what kind of focus you had in mind when you picked up *Focused Fundraising*.

- How can I avoid distractions and stay on task?
- How do I stay true to my goals with goal-oriented focus?
- How do I get calmer and more flexible in overstimulating environments?
- How do I become more centered on what I am doing while I am doing it with present-minded focus?
- None, some, or all of the above?

Typically, we have found that nonprofit professionals and volunteers just want to be less bogged down and distracted by minutiae and noise. Our own research and experience have revealed to us that the top two complaints are about messages and meetings. Tech tug. Instant overload. Distraction. These are the things that steal time from you and your work to build support for your organization and its mission.

Maggie wanted to focus on the most important elements of her job. She is adamant about her schedule. She blocks time for the tasks she views as most important. She maintains lists. She knows what her goals are. She knows what she wants to accomplish. And she goes and gets it done in the best ways she can. Yet, somehow, like so many of us, she feels that the important gets overrun by the urgent. And, at the end of the day, she feels she has not moved the dial enough. She gets burned out from time to time. Maggie follows all the *best* practices, and yet....

Maggie faces the challenge that all of us do. She wants all flavors of focus—to be goal-oriented, flexible, and present-minded. The problem is that Maggie, like all of us, is inundated with distractions. Distractions could be lowercase "d" distractions from the 4 Ms, like we've discussed. Or a distraction could be a capital "D" distraction— the kind that is unaccounted for but takes attention from all the key goals and priorities. Capital "D" distractions like interpersonal issues with coworkers, health emergencies, and family challenges can upset a delicate balance. Even more elusive are inner distractions: great ideas, surprising mood changes, obsessions, compulsions, and interests of all kinds. You know, rabbit holes, and the kind you stay up too late to pursue.

As we explore focus, we are going to talk about what focus is and what it is not. We are going to dispel some common misconceptions about focus. We are going to cover some ideas about what you can do to get more focus in your life. We will return to Maggie after we gain a deeper understanding of focus.

The Depth of Focus

Conventional approaches to develop focus often imply people are not trying hard enough, or there is something wrong with their brain. We see this as a grave misunderstanding.

Trying harder and harder to focus can lead to breakdowns. Think of conventional strategies for focus as yo-yo dieting for the brain. Consider the language we all use. "I just need to focus." "I have to block my schedule." "I just can't allow myself to get distracted." Possibly focus can be forced for weeks, months, maybe even years. However, what happens when you have bitten off too much? What happens when you cannot sleep? What happens when your schedule gets blown up, say in the event of a health emergency? What happens to focus then? A great Zen teacher, Shinzen Young, likes to ask: "What happens when the earthquake comes?"

As you know, nonprofit life is one of constant craziness. Who has room for added minor, let alone major, disruptions? We are all trying to get by with too much to do and too little time.

To be prepared to focus at all times, especially when focus is needed most, there is a way to access the core of focus rather than the typically surface advice. Depth helps reinforce the strength we all possess. For that reason, we have turned to experienced meditators and neuroscientists for guidance on focus. And experienced meditators, those who have devoted their lives to understanding conscious experience, shed light on an obvious fact: *focus develops naturally with repeated gentle attention to the breath.* That is, breathing in and out attentively fosters focus. Although this may not surprise you, is it not somewhat curious? Is it not somewhat strange that simply repeatedly attending to your breath enhances focus? We believe this finding about conscious breath practice is great news. It means that focus is an ability that can be strengthened by anyone. And it means that focus is developed more by allowing room for it than by forcing it. It taps into our resilience. Earthquakes can rock our worlds, and then we can refocus. This contradicts many popular beliefs, but it is compelling. You can focus, even in the face of constant craziness.

The common belief is that focus is about pushing harder. Coaches admonish their twitchy, restless young athletes to "Focus!" and "Pay attention." Teachers comment that "Johnny would be such a good student if he could only focus." And in the workplace, as adults, it is no different. Colleagues complain about each other's lack of focus. "He's so scattered; he's just all over the place." But rarely do we stop and ask the question: Is focus a matter of pushing harder? Is it really true that "being all over the place" is a lack of trying hard enough? What if you have little choice in the matter of focus, at least in particular moments? We will explore further the degree to which focus is voluntary.

On the opposite extreme of forced focus, some consider a lack of focus to be a medical issue. There is the widespread diagnosis of attention deficit disorder. During the pandemic, numerous studies explained the effect of loneliness and mental health on focus and worker productivity. And it is true that certain drugs have a demonstrable effect on focus. Be it caffeine or other drugs, people report enhanced focus from doses of different drugs. And so it is natural to wonder whether focus is simply a matter of biochemistry, and just a function of having the right cocktail of ingredients.

What we will present in this chapter is an understanding of focus that is not based entirely on will nor on biochemistry. We take some solace in the simple, ordinary experience of meditators throughout the ages who have found that attentive breathing can enhance focus. We have the tools right under our noses, literally. However, even if you do not have the luxury of time to take conscious breaths, you can strengthen focus in your everyday life without drugs and without trying harder. The first step, like the step Maggie took, is inquiring about what it is, especially in your own life. Recognizing that you are not focusing is part of the process to reset your thinking. With greater awareness, you can test out your understanding in practice. Reading this chapter is a great step in that direction.

Goal-Oriented versus Present Moment–Oriented

To illustrate a common misconception about focus, consider two different statements about Pat Smith.

1. Pat Smith is laser focused this fiscal year in her fundraising.

2. When she is with a donor, Pat Smith is completely focused.

These two examples illustrate the most common confusion about focus. In the first example, focus refers to Pat's long-term behaviors, the discipline of goal-oriented behavior. It refers to the fact that hard work, discipline, a clear line of sight to your goal, and a strong sense of purpose all matter a great deal to success. These effects are well-documented. Goal-oriented focus describes behaviors that take place over a period of time. Pat may be very distracted and all over the place in the moment.

In the second example, focus refers to experience in the moment with a donor. It alludes to some behaviors, for example Pat Smith's eye contact, body language, and word choice. However, the inference from those behaviors is that she is present to what is happening. In sports this is often referred to as being "locked in" or "in the zone." Pat Smith is engaging a depth of focus in the moment, which may or may not be related to the kind of focus in the first example over an extended period of time. Pat may feel alive in such an experience, but she may have little interest in the goals and discipline to sustain high performance over time. Pat may not be focused from a long-term perspective, although she is 100% there when she's with donors.

As you can imagine from just these two examples, "focus" is used to describe an array of behaviors and experiences, often lumped together. It does not help in developing focus to combine goal-oriented discipline and present-moment attentiveness. The two are related but rely on different mental muscles. It is far easier to strengthen them separately and then put them together than to keep them coupled and work on them at the same time. As you will see in later chapters, the RAISE framework maintains this separation by encouraging you to consistently set focused direction. Most of us want to be there in the moment *and* sustain line of sight on our goals for the long term. To make it clearer what focus *is*, now let's turn to what focus *isn't*.

Focus Does Not Follow Directions

Focus is not obedient. In other words, focus can be prompted but not sustained by trying harder and harder to focus.

Authority figures (like teachers and coaches) often treat focus like a disobedient child. In fact, the harder you tell yourself to focus, the more likely you are to become distracted. Perhaps more than any other simple fact in this book, realizing this can save you a tremendous amount of grief. The tech tug and instant overload will often win the battle, but you can win the peace, so to speak, if you understand the conflict.

Focus cannot be sustained by force of will alone. You do not have to take our word for it. Take a minute to try an exercise in maintaining focus without distraction.

- Assume a relaxed but upright posture.
- Close your eyes.

- Take a deep breath.
- Count silently to 30.
- Maintain exclusive focus on each breath.
- Open your eyes.

If you are like anyone we have ever met, you will not get too far into your count without some kind of distraction creeping in. It could be a physical sensation. It could be a different thought. It could be questioning "Why am I doing this?" Doubts are perhaps the greatest capital D distractions. Of course, this does not mean you can't focus, or that there is something wrong with you. This is the humbling fact that our minds keep spinning even when we want them to rest.

The claim that focus does not follow directions is not so simple. Telling ourselves to "focus" can have a momentary effect. This is why telling a kid (or colleague) to focus can sometimes work. It can be the kind of mental jump start we need to get hooked. So why is that? You can think of demanding "focus" like using jumper cables to shock your car's battery into action. The jumper cables can get the battery going, but there must be some juice left in the battery to sustain it once the cables are removed. To sustain focus, motivation has to kick in. So, for a kid (or an adult!) who is goofing off, it is better to ask about their motivation rather than yell "Focus!"

Multi-Tasking on Purpose

As a professional fundraiser Maggie could not get through a single day without multi-tasking. Tasks like responding to an email, listening for the dryer to stop, and intermittently helping your child with their homework are necessary. Given that this is the case, it is better to understand multi-tasking and focus than to chastise yourself for trying to do too much.

Multi-tasking is believed to corrode focus. But is it that simple?

In his book *The Mind Illuminated*, John Yates reveals a different way to think about focus. He explains that focus can be broad or narrow, depending on what is appropriate to the situation. The ability to zoom in and zoom out play a vital part in multi-tasking on purpose.

If you zoom out, you see that all complex skills involve multi-tasking on purpose. Consider an important meeting with a donor. There are many tasks, but one common purpose. In the meeting you are taking note of everyone's reactions. You are teeing up certain topics. You are shaping and steering the conversation toward your team's proposal. In this case your focus is broad because the situation is multilayered. If you truly mono-task, like mentally rehearsing your proposal and its key points, and do not read the room, consider people's interests, or gauge reactions to what you have said, then you will likely miss the opportunity and miss the moment.

Or consider a drummer. A skilled drummer carries out multiple rhythms with his feet and hands. Though it's many tasks to those of us who are not skilled, it's all for the same purpose. This kind of focus, best characterized in Mihaly Csikszentmihalyi's celebrated book *Flow*, is common to all of us in complex activities that absorb our attention.

The problems creep in with multi-*purposing*, not multi-*tasking*. With multiple purposes in mind, you are "half-tending" each task, as opposed to "attending" to each task. Half-tending is not about dividing attention, as commonly thought. Although it is commonly believed that attention can be divided, it is more accurate to describe it as rapidly alternating. If you ever watched the rapid head turns and wing movements of birds, you get a sense of how fast those switches can be. The alternations (referred to in a 2018 *MIT News* article titled "How the Brain Switches Between Different Sets of Rules" as "cognitive flexibility") are in fact so rapid that they are like the refresh rate on a flat-screen monitor. Though the image appears to be solid, the pixels are refreshing in microseconds, faster than the eye can see. Similarly, if you are in a meeting and going through your messages, your attention alternates rapidly between an email and something another meeting attendee said. Half-tending is taxing because the activities do not share a common purpose. It is why it is common for busy team members to get to the end of the day and say, "I have no idea what I did today."

Is it bad to half-tend? To multi-task? Well, perhaps it is rude to others if they catch you. But can you swing it? Can you be like the drummer, effectively in command of multiple rhythms at the same time? Can you zoom in and zoom out appropriately? Surely a fundraiser at a gala event has to engage this kind of flexible focus. We are not recommending that you do this all the time. You will probably see better results and feel calmer if you can somehow avoid half-tending all day. But if you have to, you might as well own the reality and get good at it.

Focus Is Not About Avoiding Bad Stuff

Juggling to avoid dropping balls is anxious juggling. Juggling to keep lots of balls in the air—that's focused juggling.

Malcolm Gladwell's *Blink: The Power of Thinking Without Thinking* reveals why so many of us are anxious jugglers. We have biases, like avoidance, that drive distraction. George Lakoff suggests in *Women, Fire, and Dangerous Things: What Categories Reveal About the Mind* that our brains and our very language to communicate are wired to collect, remember, and avoid painful memories. There's little doubt that we are biased to avoid pain, as evolutionary biologists assert.

Constantly avoiding bad stuff is one of the reasons nonprofit professionals struggle to focus. The disproportionate concern over the anecdotal—something we are biologically inclined to do—means we fall prey to the 4 Ms. We look at every text, glance at every email, and attend every meeting. We want nothing to fall through the cracks. We have FOMO about missed conversations. We often want to be "in the room where it happened" even when an after-the-fact update would be fine. As long as we strive to avoid bad stuff rather than achieve desired results, sustained focus may be unavailable.

Avoiding bad stuff is natural, and it's long-lasting. Chris remembers an encounter 20 years ago with an irate volunteer. The volunteer ranted about Chris's team and chewed him out. The volunteer's voice still rings in his ears. Chris remembers to this day the cubicle in which he sat and the look on the volunteer's face. The results of that encounter cut deep. Due to risk aversion, it's easy to have experiences like this drive endless checks, double checks, and triple checks that derail focus. Individuals go into protection mode and write "angry donor policies" and policy by exception, as we discuss later. The costs of these reactionary tactics can make focus nearly impossible.

Focus Is Not Always Laser-Like

Focus requires mental energy, but not as much you think. If it did, Netflix would be out of business.

Focus has generally been lumped together with concentration. The dominant metaphor for focus is a laser beam. A laser's intensity gives the impression that focus requires intense mental energy. This is not really true, though. If this were the case and one needed intense energy to focus, why would it be so easy to binge-watch Netflix? How could you mentally track the characters and plot lines of so many different stories?

You might argue that binge-watching Netflix is not focus since you are not getting anything done. Passive entertainment is surely different than performing a task at work, is it not? However, we would argue that it is not a different kind of focus; it's a different level of motivation. Just as easily as you can get hooked on a show, the opposite can happen. You can watch a show, space out, and have no idea what happened. The difference between entertainment and nonprofit fundraising work is that entertainment producers, writers, and directors work hard to keep your attention. But when you step from their screen to your inbox, there's no more script. In your nonprofit, you need to track the characters, the plot, and write the story.

Again, we view focus not like a fixed laser, but rather like a telescoping lens. You can zoom in and zoom out. You can go broad or narrow. So watching on Netflix is not very different from attending an important meeting or reading an email. The main difference is your motivation and whether you are interested in the subject matter and tracking what is going on.

Focus Is Not Broken by Noise

Because focus is viewed as narrowing, blocking other things out seems necessary. But is blocking out the answer?

A noisy room does not make a noisy mind. For example, some people claim they cannot focus with background noise. Others claim they must have background noise to focus. Some need "peace and quiet" to write and others, like Chris when writing his first book in 2010, needed a busy coffee shop to get down to typing. So, what is going on there? Why would noise both help and hurt, depending on who you are?

To take it a step further, some people claim that blocking times on their calendar is necessary for them to focus. Others block time but then do anything but the one thing they said they would. Why would blocking time help some people and be counterproductive for others?

Meditators and neuroscientists suggest that there can be noise *and* there can be focus at the same time. The key factor is you. Consider Maggie, involved in a key meeting with a donor at an upscale restaurant. If the meeting is in a restaurant, and there is music in the background, is it distracting? It could be if she wishes it went away. However, it could also enhance the experience if she incorporates it into the atmosphere of the meeting. This highlights a general principle, which is that it is disempowering to label something outside as a distraction. If it doesn't fit *your* soundscape, then it's a distraction. If you let it in, then focus can be sustained.

Distraction Can Enable Focus

Most everyone, even young kids, can tell when they are distracted and when they are focused. Kids can perceive distraction in their parents and teachers. Just like you can distinguish between hearing and *really* listening, or seeing and *really* seeing, you know when someone is bringing fullness of attention to you or to a meeting.

Before we return to Maggie and close this chapter, we want to show you how you can build your understanding of focus with this natural awareness of distraction. Distraction and focus go hand in hand. Consider the following three points:

1. **Distraction is not all bad.** For example, parents often distract their children from unpleasant experiences by giving them pacifiers or redirecting them to a new activity. It is a common and effective parenting decision. Similarly, who has not sought solace in a party or a puzzle to avoid real-world problems like financial trouble or health-related stress? Many days, distraction preserves sanity as much as it damages it.

2. **Purposefulness diminishes distraction.** You are ideally suited to overcome distraction because of the purpose*ful*ness you bring to causes you support. Without care and compassion, distraction can lead to purpose*less*ness. Instant overload leads you to forget your "why." A strong sense of purpose naturally diminishes distraction.

3. **Distraction has always been around.** Before the tech tug, distraction was still there. It is likely that Neanderthals went into their caves to find something and, just like us, forgot why they were there. It is natural to forget why we are doing what we are doing, in small things and big things. We believe that distractions will only grow over time as we become more reliant on devices.

To develop focus, anyone can work with distractions. Distractions can be a great reminder for focus, especially if we recognize the kind of distraction. *Unintentional distraction* is common. For example, imagine you are earnestly trying to concentrate on what you are reading right now. Meanwhile there are all kinds of things going on in the background. Sirens are going off. Your stomach is rumbling. People are walking around. Your phone dings. A TV is showing the game. At some point, the tug to find out what those other things are overwhelms your attachment to what you're doing, and so you forget it altogether. That's unintentional distraction.

Intentional distraction is when we use something that is powerfully gripping to take our minds off something we would prefer to avoid—for example, binge-watching Netflix rather than working on an unpleasant task. A very common example is putting on a podcast to avoid the boredom and discomfort of exercise. In extreme cases we use even unpleasant tasks to avoid even worse ones. Many times, colleagues during the pandemic referred to tedium at work as pleasant distractions from health concerns at home. Magicians are masters at intentional distraction, called misdirection, where they guide the audience to look at their right hand, while the left hand swiftly hides the red ball.

Training to recognize distraction helps focus and well-being. We become more mindful. The more we intentionally distract ourselves, the less we know about what is going on in our bodies. It saps us from understanding our genuine interests and desires. If you have ever wondered why you are nine episodes into a forgettable nine-season series, you know where distraction can lead.

Here is the good news. If you are good at intentional distraction, which most people are, then you can overcome unintentional distraction. You can get curious about it. You can have a good laugh about it. You can use the ability you have to intentionally distract yourself in order to avoid distraction. Of course this takes practice, but it's worth it.

Maggie's Story Continued

Maggie was a focused fundraiser before she encountered the ideas you have in front of you. Often the most focused people are the ones looking for an edge. Maggie's real edge, like yours, is that she takes the time to read and engage in genuine self-reflection. She reflects on her practices and evolves them over time. She clarifies what focus means to her. Her practices may not work for everyone; her challenges suggest that each of us must create our own path through the constant craziness. For Maggie, an understanding of focus is what matters.

What Maggie understands is that focus has more to do with purpose and interest than with force. Rather than pushing away all distractions (impossible), it is about acknowledging distractions and learning how to work with them. Rather than trying be laser-like, it is about zooming in when the situation calls for it, and zooming out when the situation calls for that. To step in and step back is the kind of flexible focus that focused fundraising is all about. Controlling the scope of attention and focus is the master skill that anyone can hone. Furthermore, Maggie knows that she does not need to tell herself to focus nor chastise herself when she goes down rabbit holes or blows off a self-commitment that had a deadline. Rather, she trusts the sincerity of her motivations and asks powerful questions about why she did what she did. She views distraction as a path to focus and self-discovery. Sometimes that distraction is the donor's attorney calling to work out a donation, as in the earlier example with Steve.

Maggie's understanding offers a better appreciation of what focus is and is not. It can be goal-oriented and present-moment-oriented. It can be flexible. And it does not need to be forced. Given a good understanding, the main asset you have to enhance focus is your curiosity. It is a far greater platform than your willpower or effort. Willpower and effort have been used for centuries to attempt to develop focus from the outside in, and they are about as powerful as the carrot and the stick. Instead, follow the guidance of Timothy Gallwey, author of the *Inner Game* series: *develop curious, nonjudgmental awareness*. Sustained focus comes from intrinsic motivations, ideally in a supportive environment. As a nonprofit professional like Maggie, connected to a mission and purpose, you are ideally suited to develop it.

■ ■ ■

You have now completed the first section of *Focused Fundraising*. By recognizing the constant craziness, elevating the value of fundraising, engaging mindfulness, noticing the tech tug and instant overload, and gaining a deeper understanding of focus, you have all the background you need to explore the RAISE framework. Curiosity and self-reflection are your best aids to face today's challenges. As you will see, the RAISE framework helps you find focus without forcing it.

PART

II

Focus-First:
The RAISE Framework

Now THAT WE have discussed the many challenges to being able to focus, it is time to start talking about solutions. In this section, we introduce you to the RAISE framework, the heart and soul of *Focused Fundraising*.

RAISE stands for:

- **R**ecognize your point of view
- **A**ssess your standards
- **I**nspire your efforts
- **S**tructure your work
- **E**volve your approach

RAISE is powerful because it helps you set focused direction for yourself and your team. We emphasize focused direction because none of us can escape overload and distraction from time to time. The tech tug and the 4 Ms are ever-present. So how do you remain focused? To focus without forcing it, we all need to believe that we are generally heading in the right direction. So, focus becomes a question like: Are we generally going in the direction we set out? When we set a direction for ourselves, can we follow it? Do we? That's where RAISE comes in.

A focus-first mentality underlies RAISE. Too often, we are all action-first. We check messages and scroll through apps without a clear why. We go to meetings without a stated purpose. The tech tug and the 4 Ms make it easy to be action-first. However, to focus-first means to develop a habit of setting direction for yourself routinely. As a habit, it means that if someone asks you why you are checking your messages, why you wrote a particular message, or why you said this or that at a meeting, you can answer confidently.

The RAISE framework was developed based on brain and behavioral science research, mindfulness practice, and direct experience with nonprofit professionals and volunteers. Chapter 7 will give you a general overview of RAISE, how it helps with prioritization, and how it deals with the vague demands of constant craziness. The following chapters will each take one of the five phases of RAISE and discuss it in more detail.

7

How RAISE Helps

GIVEN ALL THE challenges to focusing, your best bet is to consistently set focused direction. Focused direction keeps you on track, so when the tech tug or other distractions creep in, you're more likely to stick to your task. Because none of us can banish all distractions or avoid heavy workloads, the skill to master is to quickly and effectively set focused direction for yourself. Without that, it's too easy to get sidetracked and lost. Opportunities and issues stay on your mind, heightening the sense of overload. By learning the practices in this section, you can more quickly set focused direction for yourself. Focused direction is the sweet spot between goals and actions. For a project underway, it's the moment you see a path to completion. For a problem you're mulling over, it's when you land on a clear next step. If identifying a next step is difficult, it's usually because the direction is not focused enough. Without focused direction, it's easy to be overloaded by open-ended goals and ambiguous needs. The more vague demands hanging over your head, the more likely you are to get burned out. Learning how you set focused direction is what these practices are all about.

Focused Direction

Focused direction means direction you can follow. Without it, it's easy to get lost in the spin. For example, the big items linger on our lists, while the small ones get done. Routine meetings happen, but important ones don't. Small projects move forward, but meaningful ones stall out. To illustrate the difference between vague direction and overly specific direction, let's review a simple parable about asking three different people where the nearest gas station is when you do not have GPS. As you will see in this parable, there are quite a few subtle clues on what focused direction is and is not.

Three Requests for Direction

Imagine for a moment that you're in your car, you have no cell service, and you are running low on gas. Thankfully, you see someone standing on the side of the road whom you can ask for directions. So you pull over, roll down your window, and clear your throat. "Excuse me," you say, "can you tell me where the nearest gas station is?"

Unfortunately, the first person you ask is impatient and dismissive. She points and says, "That way—you'll find it." And she waves you off.

With directions too vague to trust, you drive a little way down the road until you see the next person.

The second person looks patient and calm. However, he is more absorbed in his world than in yours. He shares far too many details. He says: "So you want to keep heading this way, and you're going to pass a supermarket. Just past the supermarket is a stop sign. The stop sign there has some graffiti on it. It really needs to be redone. After the stop sign there's actually a sports betting place, it's blue with white trim. Once you pass that, you ..." By this time you've tuned out. He overloaded you with information. With directions too detailed to follow, you drive on until you see the next person.

The third person is friendly and looks kind. They consider you for a moment and simply say: "Continue to the second stop sign, take a left, and it'll be on your left." Grateful, you take a deep sigh and say to yourself, "Ahh, finally, some focused directions," as you wave thank you and drive off.

In the example just mentioned, only the third person gave you directions you could follow. They thought about it from your point of view, and gave you a path you could track. With constant craziness, the tech tug, and instant overload, it is often difficult to receive or provide directions we can follow.

Setting focused direction for ourselves is even more challenging than getting focused direction from others because it's rarely conscious. Of course we all do set direction for ourselves, but how mindful are we of it? Most of the time we subconsciously set direction. For example, you might receive an email that you are unsure how to handle. After you spend a restless night thinking about it, you figure out what to do. How did that happen?

Directing ourselves intentionally take practice. It begins with identifying topics that need a path forward or clear next steps. From there, it's a matter of thinking it through. RAISE, as we will see, is a practice that helps you to think it through. Over time, it becomes a new habit.

Setting focused direction for yourself is a daily challenge. You need room to practice. A few minutes to reflect on projects or responsibilities that require your direction goes a long way. The next section gives you a practical metaphor to make room so that you can put these ideas into practice. Setting direction for yourself requires that you place boundaries around life's demands—at least once in a while.

Making Room to Focus: A List, a Mob, a Waiting Line

Making room to set focused direction for yourself may be the single biggest challenge to practicing RAISE or any other strategy for a focus-first approach.

The following is an exercise to identify focus topics. So often we hear, "I just don't have time to focus. How could I possibly set focused direction if I don't have time to think?" This practice reveals priority topics, if you can carve out a few minutes. We call any need that requires direction a "topic." Topics range from opportunities to problems—basically anything that needs a path forward or clear next steps. If there are big-ticket items stalled on your list, they may be good priority topics. You also may find priority topics in notebooks, or just rattling around in your head. Here's how this works.

A List

Give yourself a few minutes to make a list of expectations or needs you "should" be focused on. It doesn't need to be written in anything fancy; any old notepad or document will do. Just write out a list and try to name everything that's tugging for a decision or direction, even if it's vague. Go as deep as you can to clear out those "back of mind" items that are on your summer list or are your long-term goals. All the items on your list are your topics. Once you are reasonably satisfied with your list of topics, move on to the next step.

A Mob

Take the next few minutes to associate your topics with people. Push back in your chair and view the topics clamoring for your attention. Imagine the people your list represents. Imagine them banging on your door, demanding answers or actions. No matter how unpleasant or frightening this may seem, it is a more accurate picture of how your brain views these demands on your attention. In the deepest parts of our brains, everything is happening at once. Take a few deep breaths if you need to. After you complete this step, you have actually added some emotional distance. You're ready to complete the final step.

A Waiting Line

For the last few minutes, you are going to round up the mob. Now envision all those people arranged into a line. You could imagine it as a lively line with everyone bustling and jostling for placement. They all want to come see you and get your attention. They still want answers and action, but they're willing to wait at least a little bit now. In the line, they have calmed down a bit. You can take a few more deep breaths too. By visualizing the line of people outside your door, you assert more of a boundary—at least mentally.

This exercise reveals topics and gives you breathing room to set focused direction. Gaining this kind of space can be a welcome relief. Some people find it helpful to do this once a week, or even once a day.

However, before stressing too much about the list of topics in front of you, we want to save you the grief from pointless prioritization of your list. Too often the temptation is to agonize over priorities. Who should be first? Who is more important? Typically, everyone in the line is important and warrants attention.

Consider this: Doing the most important thing is rarely the most important thing. Why? Trying to figure out the most important thing often prevents us from doing anything! Plus, the most important thing to do is not an observable action. It's invisible because it happens inside you. The most important thing is to develop the master skill of setting focused direction for yourself. Direction matters more because it is often difficult or impossible to know what the most important thing to do actually is. Trying to figure it out generally exhausts our limited brain capacity. Is it more important to respond to your boss or a volunteer? They're both important. When something is truly important to you, there's no question about priority.

The most important thing is to trust your intuitive knowledge on your topics. If you do that, and you adopt a focus-first mentality, then intuitively you will end up working on things that matter. You will feel that you're not just getting things done, but rather that you're getting the right things done. The ability to set a focused direction for yourself on open-ended topics is learnable and doable. It avoids empty prioritization loops and wasteful mental effort.

Remember the RAISE Mantra

Overload can be tamed, or at least corralled, just like you can mentally organize a mob waiting for you. You have the power to do so with your curiosity and imagination. You need not be stuck in an empty prioritization loop, endlessly besieged by the urgent demands or wrestling with what's most important. To return to the mental state best suited to work through topics that matter to you, and rise above the 4 Ms, a mental trick can be applied: a mantra. Throughout *Focused Fundraising*, we will remind you to "**RAISE the topic**" when you want to set a focused direction for yourself or your team. By RAISE, we mean:

- **Recognize your point of view (POV).** What is my POV on this topic? What is a clear path forward? A POV, your own, is the first step in setting a focused direction.
- **Assess your standards.** What would you accomplish if your standards were defined? You've probably heard the expression that the perfect is the enemy of the good. Chris often advises his workshop participants and clients that "97% is an A" to probe clarity on standards, and ask: What is A-level work? Clarity on standards is essential for focused direction.
- **Inspire your efforts.** How would you feel if you always acted willingly rather than forcing yourself to do things? Sometimes the work ahead can be daunting. A focused direction means appreciating what you can do rather than what you cannot. It means gaining inspiration from your mission, your colleagues, and your own vision.
- **Structure your work.** How would your work change if you had structures you felt were stable and supportive? Even small additions of structure give purpose to work and elevate everyone's performance.
- **Evolve your approach.** What improvements would you make if you learned from prior experiences, good and bad? Anticipating what is necessary and next will ensure that your focused direction does not get sidetracked when your initial plan or strategies fail.

RAISE elevates focus rather than forces it. No matter the topic, there's always room for greater focus. In the next section, we explore how to frame topics.

Framing a Topic to RAISE

In developing RAISE, we heard quite a bit about the frustrations with conventional goal-setting and problem-solving approaches. Goals are often elusive. Too often, goal-setting methods require you to know the goal when you start. But what if you see a need but do not know the goal? What if different people on the team have different goals in mind? Plus, goals often do not get at the heart of the matter. Who hasn't been in meeting after meeting talking about goals but never landing on a clear course of action? It can be surprisingly difficult to answer the question: What are we *really* trying to do? *Why* does it matter? RAISE attempts to avoid those pitfalls by starting with the most basic of basic steps: stating the topic. A clear topic identifies the area that needs a path forward.

To give you an idea of topics, here are some common ones:

- A volunteer who is frustrated by a lack of response
- A project with an unrealistic time frame
- A great training that has your wheels spinning, but no clear way to apply it

No topic is too large or too small. If it is on your mind, then it is a worthy topic. Setting a focused direction on a topic requires time to think, it is true, but it need not be a lot of time. Constructive mental effort is easier and better done with a practice like RAISE than a free-wheeling fashion with no constraints. George Lakoff and other writers covered in this book make this point over and over: work *with* the limits of our brains rather than denying them.

Even if you have the time and energy to do the thought work, there are several blockers to stating a topic. All of these can derail you from applying the RAISE framework and send you on mental sidetracks. The following are some of the challenges with framing a topic and stating it out loud or in writing:

- **Nonspecific urgency.** You feel the urgency but see no specific action. Example: "This proposal is due tomorrow and it is a total mess!" Are you supposed to rewrite it? Is it just one person's opinion? Vague urgency is a focus killer. Topic: "Report due tomorrow, it needs a rewrite, and that's not possible."

- **Amorphousness.** You sense that something needs to be done but it is big and ill-defined. Example: Your direct mail efforts seem to be tailing off, but you are lacking the data needed to really understand it. Topic: "Exploring possible changes to our direct mail efforts with insufficient data."
- **Vagueness.** You hear something as doable and yet there are no details. Example: "We need to fix the system." Similar to amorphousness, this obstacle can lead professionals to misunderstand the big picture or misdiagnose the problem altogether. Topic: "Reported system issues need active discussion to reveal if there are problems we can solve."
- **Pointlessness.** You simply do not see the value in doing something. Example: Fill out the dreaded audit report. These are the domain of many a fundraising professional's nightmares. These are the ultimate "management" distraction in the 4 Ms. Topic: "Audit report is required but seems to serve no one."
- **Misdirectedness.** You think someone else is in a better position to do something. Example: A volunteer complained to you and needs some TLC. You're tempted to do it yourself, but all those "hats" you wear and your "other duties as assigned" can be distractions from your highest order of impact. Topic: "Volunteer needs dedicated attention from someone and it's not clear who is in the best position to address their needs." As Jocelyn Kane, managing director of the Yale Alumni Fund, shared, "Good delegation can also bring focus."

Stating a topic out loud, or at least to yourself, even if you have no idea what to do about it, is the first step. In the words of David Allen, "naming it is taming it." If you are too frustrated that a situation is coming up or involving you, you will likely be reactive rather than causative, a state where you always influence the action. Keep in mind that you act on not just individual demands on your attention but feel the pressure of that mob that is demanding your time. This is the impact of the mental burden that so many of us carry through our days. Sometimes you need to state just the first topic in line, sometimes the first few, sometimes the whole list. The more often you frame and state topics crisply, the fewer items will build up. With less buildup, you'll receive greater support and more frequently experience focus without forcing it. With a topic in mind, you are ready to begin to use RAISE to set a focused direction.

8

Recognize Your Point of View

RAISE BEGINS WITH a topic. When you RAISE a topic, you're implicitly stating that it matters to you. However, seeing why it matters to you is often a result of untangling your own from others' perspectives. This is why RAISE does not start with goals, but rather with perspectives. Sometimes to stand in your own shoes, you have to put on others' first. Such is the nature of being an empathetic and thoughtful person.

For those of us drawn to cause-related work in the nonprofit space, we are unstoppably concerned with other's perspectives. Because of this natural empathy, the first of the five phases to RAISE a topic is to steady your own point of view. More often than not, our point of view on a given topic is blurred by the unconscious tendency to incorporate others' perspectives in addition to our own. As someone who cares about your organization or cause, you are likely to consider many points of view on any topic that matters. It is a natural part of the thought work involved in navigating any complex relationship or topic. Although perspective-taking and the underlying empathy are both strengths, they can actually derail focus if swirling considerations go unstated. A big part of being able to process a topic is to put yourself squarely in your own shoes, and speak from your own perspective.

Clarifying your own point of view (POV) is thought work. You may find it helpful to write your POV the first few times you attempt this process, but once you get the hang of it, you can just recline in your chair, close your eyes for a minute, put on some music, or do whatever else you do to reflect. The point is to uncover your own POV on the topic, no matter how crowded out it may be by others' demands and expectations. Investing this mental effort not only enhances your efforts to include diverse POVs with your own, but it also prevents you from wasting time in fruitless conflicts or pointless sidetracks.

Expressing a POV can come in many forms. What are your opinions, beliefs, and experiences? What are your intentions? There are no right or wrong answers; it's just that sometimes our own POV can be difficult to find amid the constant craziness of nonprofit life.

Four Key Perspectives

In order to recognize your POV, and set a focused direction on a given topic, you can engage four key perspectives, which we distilled for nonprofit life from multiple sources, including Fred Kofman's *Conscious Business* and Ken Wilber's *Integral Life Practice*. These perspectives are always present, though they are rarely stated. They are:

- **Their POV.** Who are *they* and what do *they* want? In the case of your topic, *they* could be another department or team, a group of donors, another nonprofit, or other groups clamoring for your prospects' attention.
- **Our POV.** Who are *we* and what do *we* want? For your topic, "we" could mean your team, your whole department, volunteers, or a new group of people that you have not identified before.
- **Its POV.** What is *it* and what does *it* require? On your topic, it could be a plan document, a strategy, a system, a set of rules, a set

of procedures, or anything in the context that is a part of the landscape asserting itself.

- **My POV.** Where am *I* on this topic? After considering these perspectives, typically some new options emerge. Often these perspectives get blended. How often have you heard managers talk about "we" and you are not clear if it refers to you or them? Identifying your perspective is easier when these other perspectives have been considered.

Because each of us is a complex, perspective-taking human being, it is important to know our limits. How many perspectives to consider? How broadly to think? Malcolm Gladwell's *The Tipping Point* presents a compelling case for simplicity. The brain can effectively only divide information (i.e., stimuli) into perhaps seven categories. It is the reason that U.S. phone numbers are seven digits, plus an easier-to-remember and compartmentalized country code and area code. Specifically for fundraising, one of the principal findings of how our brains work and how we function in society is that the average person can effectively manage about 150 personal connections. So considering four perspectives routinely is doable, as long as we keep the numbers of people involved manageable.

Steadying Your POV

Taking a moment to consider your subject and background is necessary to produce a good photo. Similarly, including the context and considering different angles steadies your own POV.

Ordinarily, perspective-taking is done subconsciously. It is rarely thought about intentionally and rarely spoken aloud. However, by going through the first step in RAISE you will find that you have a steadier POV. To establish your POV, let's take a common topic: a difficult coworker who pushes back when you ask for something to be done.

Imagine that you have a difficult coworker Ron Jones. He appears to be frustrated at meetings and monopolizes the conversation whenever you bring up certain needs. He is an important operations team member who pushes back frequently about your fundraising team's needs. To begin to apply RAISE, we describe the four perspectives.

Topic: Ron Jones

Their POV: Who are *they*? In this case, you determine that *they* are the operations team. They are amplifying Ron's concerns so that they are not working effectively with you at all any more. *They* move slowly and don't do enough in your opinion, and do not seem open to your ideas.

Our POV: Who are *we*? You determine that *we* refers to your boss and your other colleagues who know Ron and the operations team well. From this POV, you determine that *we* are looking to educate Ron and the operations team on why what you're asking for is crucial and to get them to move forward on it.

Its POV: What is *it*? You determine that *it* refers to the database and system changes you need to realize some of your goals. The system needs and the pace of change (or lack thereof) are what's really at issue.

My POV: Where am *I* on this topic? Having thought about it, you take a deep sigh and realize you are looking to move on from this as quickly as possible. Someone has to deal with it. You think that might mean bringing up the elephant in the room—**We need very different views on how changes and new apps should get approved and move forward.**

Recognizing your POV may be enough to give you a focused direction. It hinges on how big a topic it is and how much clarity you need to take action. In this example, your POV became clearer, but it remained a general direction. To make it a focused direction, you would need to answer the question of how to approach Ron about changes and new apps. As it stands, you could go down many different roads with that general direction. The subject of the next step in RAISE helps to take general direction and make it more focused. It's about clarifying standards.

Pro Tip 1: When you take this first step in RAISE, you can start with Us, Them, or It. However, we do not recommend starting with your own POV. We find that it is best to save that for last. By the time you have considered others', yours starts to form more naturally.

Pro Tip 2: Often the trickiest POV is "Theirs." Viewing situations in an unnecessarily adversarial way is common, as though a coworker, donor, or volunteer is against you rather than with you. Often, in performing this first step, you will find that "Us" can include an individual or group you previously thought as of as "Them." If you find that your mental categories do shift, you have taken a very significant step forward. Often, a focused direction is the result of removing emotional blocks, like frustrations or resentments around "us" or "them."

Pro Tip 3: Although there are four POVs, including your own, you may get a composite picture at once. Once you practice, this may take very little time. Remembering it may be enough. The point is not to belabor each POV, the point is to give yourself focused direction so you're likely to stick with it.

9

Assess Your Standards

IN THE PREVIOUS chapter, we discussed how you can recognize your POV without overcomplicating it. Most importantly, recognizing your POV involves untangling your POV from others'. In this chapter, we cover the next obstacle to focus without forcing it: unclear standards. Unclear standards almost always lead to overload and distraction.

For example, in Chapter 8 we explored a situation in which a coworker pushed back about changes involving new apps or data. After clarifying POVs, there was a general direction to approach this coworker rather than ignore the topic. But how? What to say? To use the RAISE process, the key next step is to look at standards. What are the standards for new apps and changes involving them? What's a good standard for approaching a difficult colleague? What would be a good way to handle this? Why? Stating topics, recognizing POVs, and talking about standards leads to a highly focused direction. We do not believe there are cookie-cutter answers or formulaic ways to approach coworkers or establish business practices; it's more that the habit of recognizing POVs and assessing standards provides greater focus. It may take a bit more time up front to reflect, but the outcomes are worth it.

In this chapter we will zoom out to discuss the standards for nonprofit fundraising that many organizations apply. By invoking these standards, we are not stating that industry standards are always the right ones, simply that assessing standards leads to greater focus. For example, if you believe your team is operating below industry standard on costs per dollar raised, you likely view that as a problem and seek to fix it. If, rather than cost per dollar raised, I am using a standard of return on mission to judge your team, I may view your higher than average industry cost as perfectly acceptable. As we recognize our POVs and assess our standards, we are much more likely to set a focused direction together. Although essential for focus, in our experience, this kind of alignment of standards discussion is rarely explicit.

This chapter will invite you to examine common standards for fundraising. It will also encourage you to reflect on the cognitive limitations in defining, stating, and evaluating standards. Open conversation about standards allows for a more diverse set of perspectives. Although it may seem like it takes more time, it ultimately helps you focus by avoiding distractions from tech tug and 4 M's.

Common Pitfalls to Establishing Standards

Assessing standards requires a high degree of mindfulness. In many ways, mindfulness practice is about simply noticing standards. How do we judge success? How do we decide what's good or bad? Often, standards are invoked subconsciously, and, as is well documented, with ample unconscious biases. A healthy skepticism is warranted.

Can we identify standards without biases? Daniel Kahneman's seminal *Thinking, Fast and Slow* reveals how biases affect all kinds of judgments. He describes two systems of thought. "System 1 thinking" is fast, primordial, and preattentive. "System 2 thinking" is, you guessed it, slower and more reflective. Awareness of both is necessary to avoid faulty assumptions about standards, biases, and "spotlighting" attention on the negative. We are wise to assume we enter situations with bias rather than we are somehow immune.

Are we good with quantitative standards? John Allen Paulos's *Innumeracy* highlights a human inability to comprehend big or complex numbers and their relative meanings. Consider the classic "Quarter

Pounder problem." The fast-food restaurant A&W ultimately abandoned their one-third-pound burger because most people thought it was *smaller* than a McDonald's Quarter Pounder!

Are we good at judging our abilities? The Dunning-Krueger effect reveals that we overestimate our capacity to understand complex subjects. In short, we deceive ourselves unknowingly, especially when we know less and less about the topic, as explained succinctly in Tavris and Aronson's *Mistakes Were Made (but Not by Me)*. All of these areas highlight the traps, trials, and tribulations we face when digging into our standards.

Clear standards rely on clear thinking. Kahneman, Paulos, and Tavris and Aronson suggest that clear thinking is scarce, especially when time is scarce. For instance, Kahneman provides evidence around the human tendency to anchor decisions in irrelevant numbers. Why do we build prospect portfolios of a certain size? A gift officer's ability to remember and use key relational facts about prospects shrinks as the portfolio size grows. So, for instance, the grandkid's name for a gift officer's 197th prospect is harder to retain, making the relationship less meaningful and making it much less likely that the prospect's perspective could be adequately considered. In *The Overflowing Brain*, Klingberg would effectively suggest that your brain "is full." Gladwell goes further to show that social and cultural considerations play a role, too. In addition, our limitations are exploited by the makers of all the shiny, blingy, dopamine-inducing social media tools we have in our hot little hands, aka the Tech Tug. (For a detailed understanding of what is happening here, check out Robert Lustig's *The Hacking of the American Mind: The Science Behind the Corporate Takeover of Our Bodies and Brains*.)

Common Standards for Measuring Fundraising Performance

Sometimes day-to-day standards are easier to define than the big picture. Small things to check off the list—making a stewardship call or sending that handwritten note—can really feel good. As *6 Minutes Wrestling with Life* author John Passaro quipped: "Just do the next right thing. Then repeat indefinitely." This is good, but often hamster-wheel-inducing advice, since there are typically too many right things to do on any given day. Since there are too many "next best things" to choose from, let's zoom out and look at the big-picture standards for fundraising.

The nonprofit industry has a few glowering, overarching indicators of success that are likely more a by-product than a determinant of successful fundraising. In particular, the first two indicators—total dollars raised and cost per dollar raised—in the following list seem easy to use in establishing standards, yet each has its pitfalls. They do not adequately account for donor behavior, nor do they allow room to expand investment. The second two, return on mission and engagement scoring, do a better job at describing the current state and encouraging a more focused future state.

Total Dollars Raised

"How much money did we raise?" This is generally easy to understand. Of course, definitions vary. One team's "raised" is another's "committed" is another's "attained" is another's "produced." The "when" and "what" of fundraising results seems to be the most likely to have multiple interpretations. Despite efforts by the Council for Advancement and Support of Education and the Association of Healthcare Philanthropy to define what should be counted for fundraising campaigns, there remain large swaths of unique approaches to counting dollars raised in the nonprofit space. And then there's the complication—what did it cost to raise it?

Cost per Dollar Raised

The corollary to how much was raised is this measure of purported efficiency in raising money. This measure suffers from a host of challenges, not the least of which is the hugely different circumstance that each nonprofit may experience while being expected to calculate and compare this ratio identically to other organizations. Good literature on the topic and the potential for better measures is found in Dan Palotta's Charity Defense Council. As Chuck McLean and Suzanne Coffman from Guidestar (now Candid) shared in a 2004 blog entry,

There is no question that nonprofit organizations have an obligation to manage their finances responsibly. There is also no question that ratios can be valuable tools for evaluating charitable groups. By themselves, however, these figures can be more misleading than helpful.

Return on Mission

Andrew Urban's book *The Nonprofit Buyer: Strategies for Success from a Nonprofit Technology Sales Veteran* introduced the idea of "return on mission." Return on mission offers an alternative to overly restrictive measures. Urban evaluated his experiences in Advancement technology and thought that one way to redirect nonprofits' focus was to change the metrics they use. Urban is a long-time advancement technology leader who, in his childhood, learned the importance of philanthropy as a pastor's son. Urban sought to address the "nonprofit starvation cycle," first explained in depth by Ann Goggins Gregory and Don Howard in the *Stanford Social Innovation Review*. This cycle illustrates a pattern of nonprofits that generate restricted revenue, which force them to invest too little or spend too much. Generous gifts sometimes lead to staffing decisions that cannot be maintained if the funding ceases. All the while, the drumbeat of "low overhead" plagues these groups. Urban's advice: Change the measure to change the focus, and then see the outcomes. It is smart and it aligns with SMART goal-setting practices. See Figure 9.1.

Be SMART about it: A quick note about metrics and goals. A convenient way to think of any management-level metrics and goals is to ask if they are "SMART." That is, are the metrics specific, measurable, achievable, relevant, and time-bound? Chris often encounters organizations whose goals fill a page or two yet miss out on measures that matter most. This well-worn tactic stemming from the early 1980s helps evaluate your metrics to ensure they help you achieve your goals.

Figure 9.1   SMART Goals to Help You Focus

The shift Urban suggested requires using return on mission as the primary measure of success. Return on mission is different from impact-per-dollar evaluations. Return on mission focuses nonprofits on whether their work and philanthropic results help their constituents and their causes. Does the work have the intended effect? If, for example, you strive to end homelessness and your fundraising efforts in a year help 2,000 people move into permanent homes, celebrate the 2,000 people and keep the necessary context of what that means. What does it mean to those individuals? Their communities? The world? Urban's model is similar to appreciative inquiry, in which you "map the positive core" as a way to discover even greater purpose in the work. This level of purposefulness challenges nonprofit starvation. You might even flip the question on overhead to ask whether even more overhead (literally, in this home-finding scenario) would bring your organization closer to attaining your mission. If so, add overhead. This will actually break the nonprofit starvation cycle by impressing funders and keeping them engaged. Since fundraisers work in a space that does not have the same profit motive as the for-profit world, unwittingly using the same ROI-style measure can be a detriment. Of course, this does not suggest that a team should completely eschew those other perspectives, but certainly Urban has come up with a compelling way to adjust your thinking about the high cost of low overhead. And, along the way, return on mission will certainly help you better handle distractions and establish better overall focus as it favors investment and making more time available for fundraising to support the mission.

Engagement (or Sometimes Retention)

The nonprofit industry is moving toward an emphasis on engagement, with the point of retaining relationships and donors. In higher education organizations, alumni participation as donors to their alma maters has dominated many shops, as a result of this measure's use in *U.S. News & World Report* rankings. More recently, the Council for the Advancement and Support of Education (CASE) has established a four-tier set of engagement principles that take into account softer connections like social media interactions and event attendance. These may get at the longer-term alignment of organizations with their constituents, but they sure are hard to calculate!

Jay Le Roux Dillon's dissertation, "Factors and Characteristics of Alumni Role Identity: Implications for Practice in Higher Education Fundraising and Alumni Relations," presents a series of compelling analyses on why and whether constituents may want to engage with their alma mater. His findings suggest that social media strategies can increase the "alumni role identity of graduates," as well as overall fundraising results. This is germane to focused fundraising for a few reasons. First, this means groups like CASE have added new digital engagement metrics to measure success for nonprofits, requiring all of the mechanics necessary to track them. Second, this means that nonprofits should be actively engaging their constituents in their own version of the Tech Tug, competing with TikTok, Facebook, and Google for their focus.

A challenge with these standards is that, except for engagement, they are typically lagging indicators, particularly total dollars raised. Chris was reminded of a picture-perfect example of this when he and a colleague sat in on a client's advancement team meeting. Chris's colleague worked as a fundraiser at the client more than five years earlier. In the meeting, the vice president announced a large gift, a realized bequest, from a donor formerly assigned to Chris's colleague. Amazingly, there had been no new visits to the prospect in the previous five years, just good stewardship of the original solicitation. Bottom line: the person in the room most responsible for the gift had not worked at that institution in over five years! Fundraising is a team effort and can take years to come to fruition.

The cost per dollar raised can be a similarly shallow standard. The lack of investment that this often triggers frequently leaves organizations in the nonprofit starvation cycle mentioned earlier. What is generally missing from these standards is an approach that is mindful of your organization's situation. Maybe it makes sense for the next five years for your organization to heavily invest in infrastructure or add in new team members whose productivity will not result in new gifts for a year or two. There is a reason, for instance, that far too many nonprofits have little to no sustained planned giving effort despite the trillions of dollars that will be transferred from our donors' estates in the next few decades. The sad fact is that realizing those bequests "takes too long" for far too many unfocused nonprofits. And the same "need-it-this-year" imperative can derail you if unspoken standards and incentives are in place. Nuance and inspiration crash head-on into the buzzsaw of conformity that these standards force upon unique institutions.

Best Practices versus Practices That Work Best

Professionals can learn from their peers. We are no different. We base our guidance on in-the-field discussions, survey data, organizational assessments, and research. But "best practices" are frequently misleading because they often do not fit the specific circumstances.

Do not aspire to follow *the* model team or model standards. Instead, aspire to create *your* model team using *your* standards with inspiration from the so-called best. Chapter 19 presents a novel approach, dubbed the *Focused Fundraising Maturity Model*, that can be used to guide an organization toward an increasingly focused environment. It includes recommended practices but encourages organizations to be realistic about their stage on the maturity model in order to determine which standards fit.

In *An Executive's Guide to Fundraising Operations*, Chris argued that rather than "best practices," one should seek "practices that are best":

… I had a discussion about best practices for a fundraising operations team, and it was not going as well as I had hoped. The group was clearly anxious about my presence, which I always understand at the beginning of a visit, but this was well into the discussion. I wanted to understand the feelings in the room, so I asked: "You guys seem agitated. Is there something we should discuss?" The response was unexpected: "We need to keep copies of checks!" This was unexpected because we had not been discussing checks and copies, just general gift processing steps. However, this group had participated in a "best practices" discussions where the presenter stated that, because the IRS does not require nonprofits to keep checks, their university would be expected to follow suit and stop copying checks.

Now, I am in favor of streamlining processes and saving trees. And there are alternatives to some of the photocopying practices I see. These options include lockboxing and receiving images from your bank or implementing an onsite document imaging approach. However, I am never in favor of applying "best practices" without assessing the unique components of an organization's fundraising environment ....

The main message here is that best practices may not apply, or may only partially apply. As a fundraising executive, you should be careful about the resources necessary to attain certain practices. You should adopt practices that are best for your institution to generate best results. (Cannon's *An Executive's Guide to Fundraising Operations*)

A decade after writing this passage, no part of that book has garnered more commentary. Dissenters claimed: "Of course you need to take other factors into account, but without 'best practices,' we cannot be sure we have the right policies and procedures, and our measures of results need outside context." While the context piece is true, it proves the point that a shared, often overly ambitious, and even naïve set of standards is often misguided. Context is derived at the organization level or the individual level; that is, it is *your context* that matters most. Comparing yourself to others to gain clarity and develop strategies can create the alpha logic problem we discussed earlier. This is similar to the problem of trying to "keep up with the Joneses." It can too often result in the opposite effect—more distraction, more noise, and less attention to what is really important for your situation. Keeping up with the Joneses at work is just as counterproductive as it is at home. And a "presence is productivity," "metrics only" work arrangement is equally counter to establishing the level of real purpose and focus most teams need. This has become even more clear as many organizations are facing a paradigmatic change in the work force, ushered in by the so-called "Great Resignation" in 2021.

Take, for example, "best practices" for higher education. Rumor has it that CASE stands for "copy and steal everything," implying that one organization should borrow liberally from their peers. While higher ed shops tend to share generously, the danger in reading too much into programs like Voluntary Support of Education Survey (VSE) reporting is that you can easily be distracted by what your organization does not have. Spinning up programs for giving days and other alumni-focused engagement practices may make no sense for your organization. Often the noise and shiny objects that influence us and our boards result in well-intentioned, ill-suited efforts that distract us further. For instance, newer, urban public universities very often raise 50% or more from their communities and specifically the corporate community. These data fall well outside the "best practices" at elite liberal arts colleges and are even more askew to the *GivingUSA* data patterns, which show that "individuals" do almost all of the giving each year. Should these urban public universities change their practices despite their experiences and prospect pools? Hardly. You can learn from others, but learning what works for you is the real goal. It's *your* standards that matter.

Knowing Your Standards Means Avoiding Noisy Data

Daniel Kahneman, author of *Thinking, Fast and Slow*, reminded us in a *New York Times* article in May 2021 that it's not just bias, but also noisy data that challenges us individually and as a society. In "Bias Is a Big Problem. But So Is 'Noise,'" he was distinguishing between bias and noise to ensure that both are taken into account. In his subsequent 2021 book, *Noise*, he further shared that bias is like a scale that always provides a too-high or too-low weight. Noise, on the other hand, is like a scale that is randomly wrong in either direction. Both mislead.

In the world of fundraising, where nearly every act of significant charity is itself somewhat of an anomaly, zeroing in on the most meaningful standards is vital. One person who has started to master this complex space is Nathan Chappell. Chappell runs DonorSearch's Aristotle data analytics arm. We visited in 2021 to discuss how data and complex computations can be used to help make sense of the noise. In the early days of custom predictive model building, Chappell learned the hard way that building complex machine learning models can be quite expensive in time, resources, and budget. While working for a leading cancer center philanthropy team, it was common for him to spend close to $100,000 per model and wait months for results. And the predictive scores on their own were not always likely to sway gift officer behavior or researcher prioritization. Today, data integration, computational power, and availability of advanced statistical packages means the same work can be accomplished in days and for a fraction of the cost. In recent years, significant advances in artificial intelligence and visualization tools have advanced efforts to put this data to work. Yet this does not change the potentially distracting aspects of data analytics output; that is, even though much-improved analytics can produce clearer results, we still need to make good choices and decipher the signal from the noise. Chappell is convinced that computational power plus understanding the sector will aid those choices.

Our models are not immune to biases and noise. For instance, maybe you are convinced that the research team always overestimates capacity scoring and so you discount their guidance (a show of bias). Or, maybe your average results from major giving solicitations appear solid, on average, but upon closer inspection, you find that your realized gifts are sometimes much lower than expected and sometimes higher than hoped (a demonstration of noise). Instead of examining the cause for the wide swings in results compared to expectations, you might not recognize the noise in the data, leading to a false sense of confidence in future planning and efforts. Chappell's work focuses on making all of the available statistical analyses as meaningful as possible.

Along with handling the potential distractions inherent in AI and big data, Chappell shared down-to-earth advice on focus as many of us continue to wrestle with the shifts occurring in our work environments: "During the pandemic, I started to clock in and out of work, which provided much needed boundaries between work and life. Knowing that I would deliberately leave my desk and office behind at a certain time allowed me to ultimately get more done. It also allowed me to come into my office with purpose and focus." So here is a professional at the top of his game dealing with terabytes of data and potential distractions at every turn, yet he has been mindful enough to add some structure to his day to avoid overload.

■ ■ ■

If you take the time to assess your standards, you stand a better chance of routinely setting focused direction. Whether it's on big topics like team performance or small topics like handling a specific donor, talking openly about standards gives you meaningful gauges. It helps you define what success looks like. It helps you know what it means to get the job done. Importantly, it helps you avoid the distraction and discouragement of adopting best practices that do not fit your context. We continue on with RAISE, to inspire our efforts.

10

Inspire Your Efforts

Choose to spin rather than be spun.
—A slogan for us throughout the pandemic

IN THIS CHAPTER, we discuss inspiration. Rather than the typical view of inspiration based on positive motivation, we emphasize the awareness of "interference," as Alan Fine describes in his book *You Already Know How to Be Great*. According to Fine, interference is all the stuff that gets in the way of what you want. As you saw from the first two chapters on RAISE, major interference comes from an unclear POV and from unclear standards. One of the most common forms of interference is anxiety about falling behind. How do you feel good about a day's worth of work, when at the end of the day your inbox has more messages and your to-do list is longer than it was when you started? Without clear standards on being "caught up," revving yourself up with positive motivation and "thinking positive" often just fuels the constant craziness.

So rather than emphasizing positive motivation, we encourage you to acknowledge bad stuff and all kinds of interference. Given that our brains are wired to give the negative stuff greater attention, this saves precious time and energy from denying it. Plus, acknowledging the challenges is all part of getting in touch with your POV. All of us want to feel good about cause-related work, so if there's a lot of interference it's best to get it out in the open. To gather inspiration, even with lots of interference, this chapter offers several metaphors and practices drawing on a rich tradition of creative and interactive pursuits, like improv and music. Inspiration does not have a plug-and-play solution. Rather, by acknowledging interference and engaging your curiosity it seeps in gradually, day by day.

Bright Spots

We all know that nonprofit life is challenging. Accomplishments of any kind are challenging. So, for inspiration, we focus on changes that make significant effort worthwhile. Looking for "bright spots," as Dan and Chip Heath call them in their book *Switch*, is a way to expand motivation, even when times are challenging. It is the bright spots that give us hope and fuel our sense of meaning. How do we give some attention to them?

Looking for bright spots does not mean ignoring dark clouds. Typically, skepticism and doubt keep us in our comfort zone rather than in our learning zone. Our learning zone is awkward and uncertain. Rather than pushing doubt aside, though, looking for bright spots is a way to have a balanced point of view. Why ignore encouraging signs? Why overweight doubt? It is distracting and misleading to only consider discouraging signs.

Bright spots can show up in the unlikeliest places. There is a wonderful scene in the movie *The Princess Bride* in which the hero, Westley, faces impossible odds to save his true love, Princess Buttercup. He is temporarily paralyzed from the neck down, and he needs to break into the locked castle and overcome 60 guards. He has two friends with him, and he asks them to list their assets and liabilities. After they list them all, he gets momentarily discouraged and says, "if we only had a wheelbarrow ...." Turns out, his friends had forgotten to mention the wheelbarrow, thinking it was not significant enough. This "wheelbarrow effect" happens all the time when we forget to look for bright spots. We seek only the evidence to support our current position, not all the available resources. It is important to allow room for wheelbarrows, even if our colleagues might not see them right away.

Looking for bright spots adds personal meaning. In *Barking Up the Wrong Tree*, Eric Barker reveals the importance of looking for meaningful motivation. Not only is it vital for results, but also for well-being. Nonprofit work is all about meaning, and meaningful work is the key to satisfaction as well as sustained focus and inspiration. As Barker writes: "Meaningful work means doing something that's (a) important to you and (b) something you're good at." In order to inspire effort, you need to tap into inner motivation, not outer motivation. Outer motivation is what the Boss or Board says. It's what you should do. Inner motivation is your own why: how you connect with the direction or goal that's in front of you. This is a habit that can be refined with practice.

Bright spots make effort worthwhile. By regularly looking for bright spots, you open up to opportunity. You routinely ask: What is changing that might make effort worthwhile? You look inward and outward. By asking what makes effort worthwhile, you are exploring the potential benefits and how they relate to your judgments. By asking about what is changing, you raise possibilities. This is a healthy form of doubt, rather than the self-defeating kind. In the *Power of Agency*, Napper and Rao offer a humbling truth, "As much as you may think you know about a given situation or problem, there is always the possibility that someone else knows something that you don't." Humbling, yes, and liberating, too. In any situation, there may be changes and choices that will make your effort worthwhile. There may be bright spots.

The Spinning Top

One way to acknowledge and thereby relieve pressure is by recognizing the whirling nature of nonprofit life. In 2011, Chris's *An Executive's Guide to Fundraising Operations* introduced the spinning top as a powerful metaphor to understanding the fast-moving nature of fundraising operations. You can engage this metaphor now. Imagine your fundraising efforts as a spinning top. In the 2011 version, the top is made up of a five key elements—data, technology, processes, reporting, and people.

Now think of people as the post that you spin right in the center. With a spin, as the top whirls faster and faster, you get the sense that one of these areas could topple the whole operation if it is out of balance. For instance, having bad data generally is a culprit. Data can always be better, whether that is defined as more copious, more accurate, more recent, more meaningful, or all of the above. For many fundraising professionals, imagining what topples the top comes back to poor business intelligence resources or perhaps onerous business processes. The top may wobble due to weak prospect portfolios or a shaky case for your campaign. The idea is that, when using this technique, a professional fundraiser can often quickly isolate the root causes of the wobbles.

Ten years later, we expanded the metaphor—choose to spin, rather than be spun—which illustrates the point of *Focused Fundraising*. It ties into the idea of "spinning forward," which essentially means if you need to spin the top, be mindful of the spinner.

A terrific example of the power of the spinning top metaphor took shape at a health care organization in the Midwest. The setting was a new foundation president seeking to gain an understanding of why operations appeared to be so ineffective. This new leader's take was that reports were lacking and incomplete. There was little insight into the programs and their progress. This assessment was mostly on point, except that it described the symptoms—no good reporting—and not the root cause—outdated technology. In this case, the limited reporting tools in place resulted in either horribly inefficient Excel pivot tables or awfully dated and inflexible programmed reports in the form of PDFs. The frustration with reporting in this case was not misplaced, but the heuristic of the spinning top pointed to the real imbalance: outdated tech. Getting at the heart of the matter lifted some pressure.

This new foundation president did not need to understand technicalities around business intelligence resources, database fields, code issues, or other complexities. Those are details that keep great fundraisers further from their donors and prospects. Instead, the metaphor compressed a host of issues into an understandable solution: address the diagnosis, not just the symptoms. When you can distill a complex situation to parts of a spinning top, the lesson sticks.

Focus on the Top

As far as focus goes, the past decade has seen the spinning top metaphor grow and build into an even more robust explanation of what leading fundraisers consider important. Many professionals have extended the metaphor to an allegory explaining the current state of their team's woes and pointing a path to a better future. Two further additions to the spinning top metaphor make it relevant for focused individuals and teams.

First, focused fundraisers seek a smooth, uncluttered surface—a supportive environment. The surface one spins on is perhaps the most noted addition to the spinning top metaphor. As you can imagine, it is rare that you get to spin a top on a perfectly flat slab of granite. When you do, that top will spin for five to six minutes. It is impressive. But the real world does not always allow for nice smooth surfaces. This is one of the hallmarks of attaining focused fundraising levels. The table is rarely level. The surface is bumpy. Friction is a problem. For many of us, to carry the metaphor, the table is on fire, or one of the legs is missing. It is raining, or just hailed, and generally, the surface (aka, your fundraising shop) is a hot mess. That is the constant craziness of nonprofit life.

Second, a patient, dedicated spinner is a necessity. Many fundraisers suggested over and again adding the person who is spinning the top into the allegory. There are a few areas where the spinner starts to impact the metaphor. Chris can tell you that the top does not always spin perfectly for minutes at a time. It has taken some practice to get it right. Spinning (and not being spun) takes practice and discipline. In addition, the spinner is not always the same person. A professional's boss, boss's boss, or Board may have a spin. Fate and life certainly take their turns when it comes to distractions and focus in our lives. A final observation is that the spinner needs to monitor and re-engage significantly. The top is not a perpetual motion machine. It needs to be respun. It may need to be picked off of one surface (say, a sketchy staffing environment due to a board issue) and moved to another.

The purpose of the spinning top metaphor was to provide a clear explanation so leaders could turn attention to organizational priorities. Of course, whether you are a leader or individual contributor, it frequently feels like there are so many tops spinning that you are like the harried performer spinning plates at a circus. If you remember that you can be the spinner, and you can spin forward, you can keep your attention on your priorities. If you remember that spinning is a practice, you can give yourself grace when the top tumbles prematurely. The allegory of the spinning top is an easy-to-remember tool to enable focus.

Making a Choice

The spinning top distills to a central pro tip for focused fundraising: **choose wisely**. Balancing the spinning top requires effort and discipline. You choose when and where. You choose the techniques. And there are often multiple tops you might be spinning. Work. Life. Kids. Friends. Ideally, these are all spinning along nicely in our lives. Ideally, we can take the time to respin a fallen top. Ideally, the environment remains clear of debris. If the top will not spin and it is a one-time experience, just let it rip again. But, if you discover systemic issues that are disrupting the top (and you!), you need to understand them if you want to spin forward.

We also need to understand when it is acceptable for the spinning top to stop. This requires using a superpower of those fundraisers who can achieve focus: choice. A professional cannot do it all. Time is too short and choices are too numerous. What is critical is thinking about what imbalance is unacceptable. Which toppled top will have unacceptable repercussions? Which environment is simply too bumpy or which spinner needs to be avoided or trained? These are tough choices. But a focused fundraiser achieves goals through shutting out some choices and not flinching about selecting others. That text message in the middle of the day? Ignore it (but first, set a ring tone for those few loved ones whose connections demand attention). The unsolicited emails? Delete them (but first, set a business rule for the things you will read; for instance, in Chris's case, if the sender uses a ".org" or ".edu" email address, these get reviewed, whereas others go to Clutter). This book is full of encouragement to assist with the challenge of choice. Hopefully, the spinning top metaphor, much like the "big rock" story later in this book, will inspire you and take some pressure off.

Of course, some days (or even most days), one simply cannot avoid overwhelming choices to make. Good metaphors or not, the reality of, say, a 412-email day can be daunting. One way to look at this is to realize that being overwhelmed can be a consequence of success. Being overloaded in a purposely productive role can be overwhelming but it is our *raison d'être*. Read on to examine how this can be the case.

What Is Changing That Makes Focus Possible?

For inspiration, it is essential to look for what is changing. What is changing that makes focus possible? What is changing that can lead to less distraction?

Although the tech tug is real and can lead to distraction, it is not really good or bad. Often experts view the current landscape of work and life with a bias for or against technology. Is the rate of change and innovation good or bad? Is texting good or bad? Is screen time good or bad? Are bots and AI good or bad? Although there are many points of view on these matters, the issue of distraction is more like a feature that comes along with new tech and the increase of tugs on attention. And just as there's a greater tech tug, there are also more apps for wellness, for meditation, and other mindfulness practices that can help you decompress. With the pandemic there was a collective realization that we are in fact in new territory socially. New and emerging features of life cannot be addressed with yesterday's advice. Much of the "best practice" advice from leading thinkers on focus is comes from an era of desk memos and fax machines. It has not been adapted for today's conditions, which include a level of 24/7 immediacy that no era in history could possibly mirror. It is not that the wisdom and insights and history cannot offer lessons; it is just that the ways of thinking about dealing with paperwork efficiently do not necessarily apply to a world of bots and AI. Elaborate principles of decision-making may hold up if you are making six decisions a day, but fail when you are making six before you get out of bed in the morning.

You can manage interference by acknowledging what is changing, and what makes effort worthwhile. First, you can take an open-minded approach on whether technology and change is good or bad, as it is undoubtedly both. Second, you can lean into the amorphousness of focus and learn more about it. Get curious about it. And, third, you can ask what is relevant today and for today's challenges. Even more so, you can begin to wonder about tomorrow's pace, volume, and boundaries. You may find that this gives more importance to asking about what is changing, which further broadens your perspective.

An Alternative to No: "Yes, and …"

Another way to reduce interference is to get creative with how you say no. Part of focus requires being smart about what you commit to and what you avoid. As Kahneman, Sibony, and Sunstein's book *Noise* and Klingberg's *The Overflowing Brain* highlight, choice is a challenge because there is so much more of it than ever before. So why not get creative with your yeses and nos?

"No" is a powerful word. Stated well and with context, "no" can save your weekend, give you license to decline a meeting request, and otherwise gain some time and focus in your often overwhelming life. It is, though, surprisingly hard to say. "No" can be seen as being too blunt, too unsupportive, and too final. For many in fundraising, "no" feels unavailable when dealing with very generous but sometimes very demanding donors. With so much of fundraising about getting prospects to "yes"—to that proposal, to that direct mail piece, to that event invite, to that discovery meeting—an emphasis on "no" can seem impossible. But getting to "no" can be as important to a fundraiser as getting to "yes."

Camden Morse from the fundraising shop at Johns Hopkins University and Medicine suggested an alternative to "no" that stems from her improvisation experiences. In her onstage world, Camden and her colleagues sought to keep the dialogue going—to support each other. Morse is a sharp, experienced professional. Her work at two of America's largest universities belies her early career in the arts. She also practices mindfulness as a means of zeroing in on the most important elements of a situation. As a self-described academic late bloomer, her unflappable aptitude for improv made her more effective in fundraising roles, too. During a panel in April 2021, Camden highlighted the value of improv in her work:

Everyone should go out and take an improv class. You should also consider mindful meditation when working on requirements, data, and managing projects (for fundraising). These share two tenets that help you deal with the complications of our work.

The first tenet is that improv has a basic rule to say "yes and…" instead of "no." This allows you to build on the discussion and listen to people to understand their ideas and potential solutions. The second is that mindfulness helps me really be present and listen to the other person. When I go beyond thinking about what I will say next, I can better understand and help solve that person's needs. If I don't maintain mindfulness, I have left the room, at least in my head, while I go and try to solve the problem before hearing the person out.

The application of improv to focus is evident. The ability to ebb and flow through conversations, engaging your audience, never stopping the bit, always handing your peers an opening to succeed ... these all require focus and multi-tasking. You must be in the moment. You must listen to those around you and pick up on sometimes subtle cues. These cues may even be about yourself. Distractions that you cannot absorb are a killer to improv, unless you can make them part of the bit. This is where your rules and principles come in. If you are Steve, who picked up that eight-figure call one day, your rule is you always answer the phone. If you are Cynthia (who we will meet in Chapter 13) engaging with a prospective donor, you always make it personal and ask about family first. If you are handling gifts, you always look for those front-of-the-line checks. These routines can help you flow through an improvisational day without every distraction pushing you off your core mission.

For improv, "no" ends the interaction. Imagine for a minute a comedian on Drew Carey's *Whose Line Is It Anyway?* saying "No thanks, Drew, I do not want to act like a ...." "No" kills the flow. However, "yes, and ..." becomes a subtle and critical tactic to engage your colleagues, acknowledge their contribution, and redirect the dialogue toward a more fruitful topic. "Yes, and ..." is as much an artful phrase as "no" can be a stark one. And both are useful in the pursuit of focus.

"Yes and ..." riffs on wonderful insights from William Ury in his book *The Power of a Positive No.* Ury argues that you can always say yes to a relationship and no to a request. A positive no is that affirming way to say no that great improv artists have mastered. It is a no that doesn't even feel like one.

Of course, the hardest challenge with saying no is that you do not see how you can. Would it kill your reputation? Would you let your friends down? Your colleagues? Will the project go off the rails? Will others be mad at you? Would you get fired? Would there be a lawsuit? Will you get in trouble? As fundraisers, many hold the "cheerleading" myth of your job as being "nice" and "helpful" and "outgoing," all of which imply saying yes more than no. "Yes, I can help you with that newsletter (which has never proven to entice major donors to give)." "Yes, I can put that prospect research profile together (on that never-donor who appears to actively give to areas we do not even support)." "Yes, I can organize that event (that will take a month to deliver and will yield markedly less than the major giving work I had planned)." These are all too common yeses that turn a distraction into a full set of activities, further removing us from the highest order of our best, focused work. It is following a vague or overly specific direction, not a focused one.

Rather than being a people pleaser, think of focused direction like navigating the risk of wasting time. No one wants to waste time. This view is better illustrated by "yes, and …" In this view, as a nonprofit professional or volunteer, your job is to avoid wasting time using the resources you have. The resources are your prospects' capacity, your organization's mission and case for support, and your time. (Your time! What an idea! Imagine persuading your leaders, boss, and colleagues to approach time management as risk management.) The risk you are managing is the potential that any of these three items—revenue, mission, and time—are not maximized by fundraising efforts. In this way of thinking, a wasted lunch with an unqualified, uninterested, not-so-prospective donor (which perhaps you or research or a volunteer leader could have figured out) is a risk. In this approach, saying no to such ill-spent endeavors is your job. Helping you know whether or not to say no is also the job of the prospect development team and others. In this model, you can achieve greater focus saying no on some things and focusing on those opportunities where saying yes will yield greater results.

"Yes and …" removes a lot of pressure from directionless urgency. This is the promise of focused fundraising. At times, this may mean that your focus actually broadens. You may say "yes, and …" to some pretty unlikely things because you are focused on the long game and need to expand what you do in certain cases. But you can only do so if you diminish what you do in those less valuable areas. And, for this to work, mastering the "yes, and ..." will get you a similar result as a no but with all of the relationship-maintaining benefits of a yes.

Consider the often-dreaded golf tournament fundraiser. The location, the logistics, and the players all require more attention than the typical on-campus or nongolf cultivation event. Saying no just might sour things with your director, dean, or the donor who made the suggestion. Saying yes just might cost you around 5% of your total year's worth (!) of available hours to spend fundraising. How about saying yes, and ..., though? Imagine if your standard response to a request for a golf tournament is:

Yes, and ... we need to structure the fees, sponsorships, and outright philanthropy to generate a gross philanthropic revenue of at least $xxx,xxx and include a time and place for our leadership to share and present the case for support. Who will you plan to solicit for the lead support roles and how can we work [insert names of prospects you want to attend] into the foursomes?

With this approach, you will have either helped your team raise a decent amount toward your goals or persuaded the requester that their role in getting this off the ground is more significant than they thought.

As we discuss later, policy guidance for, say, gift solicitation and acceptance can help with saying no or yes, and ... in ways that minimize your risk. For instance, any fundraiser reading this needs to realize that one day, cryptocurrency and NFTs will likely be just as normal to accept as works of art or maybe even mutual funds. Should you say no to the request of a donor who wants to give Bitcoin? Of course not! Instead, say:

Yes, and ... how about we use the proceeds from your gift to first establish a policy and protocol through our legal and compliance teams to ensure that every Bitcoin gift from now on is handled as effectively as possible to support our mission? We think this will require about $xx,xxx in fees and we hope you agree that adding it to your generous gift would be a valuable approach.

In cases like these, a prepared policy can help you focus on what is next while having streamlined processes to handle what is in front of you. If you have never encountered what is in front of you, though, consider saying yes, and ... rather than yes or no to such an opportunity.

In some cases, "Yes, and ..." is really saying "Yes, if." "If" certainly competes with "no" as one of the most powerful words in the English language. "Yes, we could accept your proposal *if* ..." and then you name the terms, some of which can be stark. To look for ways you can say "Yes, and ..." or "Yes, if" is to stay open to what other people and situations present. It also values letting other people down easily. We all know what it's like to approach colleagues who seem to enjoy saying no. There are sometimes whole departments of no. No, we don't have the resources. No, it's not a priority. No, we don't have the budget. No, there's no capacity. No, it's not a good fit for us. But we can all understand a no without such a heavy hand. No does not feel like rejection or denial when our shared humanity is recognized; it feels like an *if*. To see this in action, you can turn to reality TV contest judges like those on *The Voice* and see how the judges are coached to let contestants down. One well-coached judge said: "I know you will succeed next time because of the way you handled this moment." That is saying "yes, if..." to the person and the relationship. Yes, if you come back again and show you did the work, then I will consider it. Said with sincerity, it leaves the contestant's humanity intact.

Inspiration is essential to RAISE. There's a reason it's at the center of the process, though, and not the beginning. Inspiration comes more naturally when you have a clearer POV and standards. Otherwise, it's too easy to try to psych yourself up artificially. Inspiration follows when you take a balanced view and look for meaning. Seek bright spots, recognize the spin, and moving fluidly with "yes, and ..." so you avoid costly overcommitment or risk being trapped in uninspiring activities. All of these practices allow you to build on your natural motivation. They also give you a strong mindset to structure work, the subject of the next chapter.

11

Structure Your Work

THE RAISE FRAMEWORK addresses the five phases to set focused direction. The first few phases help you address an unclear POV, nebulous standards, and artificial inspiration. Now we examine how you structure your work. This is a vast topic that could be several books in its own right. So we will boil it down to its essence: structure is highly personal.

Think of it like this. Our brains need to know that there are structures in place, or that can be put in place, to support what we are doing. Without structures, our inspiration will go to waste, like a great idea without any place to share it. Although the need for structure is universal, the structure we establish is personal. One of us likes a plan and the other likes to wing it. One of us works best under pressure and the other rehearses endlessly. To reinforce structures that work for you, we've given you a sampling from leaders in the field.

Structure Is Personal

Your career, your day-to-day, and your organization's progress are all guided by personal values and principles. There are solid industry guidelines to use, like the Association of Fundraising Professionals (AFP)

Donor Bill of Rights and CASE, AFP, and Association of Healthcare Philanthropy (AHP) guidebooks for the big picture. There is RAISE, of course, to set a focused direction amidst the constant craziness. But no matter how good a framework is, it needs to connect with you on the ground level, with your habits and tendencies. Despite similarities, no two fundraisers or fundraising shops are the same, and so all recommendations must be tailored to individual circumstances and those "practices that are best" for you.

How different are we? Well, that depends on who you ask. So, we asked industry-leading professionals to share their fundamental principles and ideas about structure and focus. What you will read here may be a mirror image of the way you tackle your challenges. You may learn some new tips. You may see a strategy or structure that simply will not fly within your organization. Let's start with a professional whose focus on major giving has helped his team increase results by around 500%.

Art Ochoa, Senior Vice President of Advancement and Chief Advancement Officer at Cedars-Sinai Medical Center

Art Ochoa is a fundraiser's fundraiser. In FY2021, his team worked tirelessly through the pandemic and raised over $200 million, a record-if-painful year due to Cedars-Sinai's valiant work during the height of the pandemic. Art got his start as a tax lawyer and then as a planned giving professional. He moved into the lead development role at Cedars-Sinai just as the organization was professionalizing its fundraising efforts. The move from many to fewer events, less to more data-driven strategies, and more and more major and principal giving closely follows the Major Giving Maturity Model found in Chapter 18. Despite his organization's deeply capable constituency, the growth of philanthropy was not a foregone conclusion. Fostering philanthropy required tremendous vision and guidance.

Art's approach to his work has always been focused. Chris has worked with Art and his team since the 2000s. Throughout that time, Art was not an ever-present participant in Chris's consulting engagements with the Medical Center. That was a good thing. That was an indication of Art's focus. Instead of spending significant time with Chris tinkering on topics around prospect management and related operational efficiency, Art was "focused on closing gifts." "The challenge of prioritizing has always been there," Art shared, "but it is more pronounced now" due to the digital distractions we all face.

These days, he prefers texting those in his portfolio once he gets to know them. His assigned prospects seem to prefer it, too. He claims no special tricks or tips, yet he was very clear about how he organized his time. "I will adjust my schedule as needed, every day. I don't want to be rude or insensitive with colleagues, but if I can make better use of my time, I will shorten meetings." His lawyering days, when he tracked his work "six minutes at a time," etched into him an emphasis on optimizing his time. The results have largely spoken volumes. He has helped Cedars-Sinai increase giving by over 500% since taking his role.

His advice for those who are busy, young fundraising professionals boils down to focusing on the most important areas. He shared that "in everyone's job description, the list of responsibilities is always a mile long. Of those, there are about three or four things that if you do them well, you might get that promotion or a better salary. There are also a few things that could get you fired if you don't handle them well. Do those things well, but try to avoid or ignore the rest." He added that measuring too many things amounts to less insight than expected and that you should avoid such traps. This is sage guidance from someone who has expanded his impact by value engineering his daily focus and filtering out the noise to close more gifts.

Blaire Atkinson, President of the Oklahoma State University Foundation

Blaire Atkinson's approach to information overload and distraction mirrors what a lot of us do: She dug in, muscled up, and worked more hours. She woke up earlier and got to work before sunrise. Her role now is a little less frenetic than her previous one, where she served as the interim president for the Oklahoma State Alumni Association while serving as the Foundation's new president! At the time, the transformational situation at the Association, which had just switched its funding and membership model, required her leadership to ensure the success of these big-ticket changes. Knowing Atkinson is to know she wanted to see them through. But the Foundation role needed to be filled, too, and it was a great opportunity. What is a professional fundraiser to do? Both jobs, apparently.

Atkinson managed both roles for about six months, handing over the Association reins just in time to have COVID upend her plans and require completely different strategies and execution in her first 18 months leading the Foundation. Atkinson's approach to the tech tug and the potential to be overloaded also mirrors some of what Ochoa shared. She is a deft communicator. She is quick to text if appropriate. Managing and sticking to her calendar is clearly important. She also leveraged early on the deep reservoir of support inherent in the Foundation's culture. The Foundation is a group of focused professionals. They live their values every day. Part of Atkinson's focus and ability to function with her workload stemmed from the "great people" around her.

One of Atkinson's secret weapons to allow time to focus is something she calls "blind trust." It is an outcropping of the Foundation's great culture. She has team members in whom she has placed deep and abiding faith. She knows that she and her colleagues are aligned at their cores. Chris Campbell, senior associate vice president of information strategy at the Foundation, is one of those partners in whom Atkinson places such trust. "Delegation is not a strength," Atkinson shared, but she is willing to completely rely on her team for the things they do best. In this case, the organization is moving from a legacy system to an innovative advancement technology ecosystem. Campbell is leading the tech transition with her full support. Her strategy there is telling and affirms the trust she places in her team: in essence, she is not involved in the day-to-day of this technology transition, although she will dive in and discuss whenever asked or needed. Her trust and hands-off approach have allowed a crop of team members to grow and build skills in ways never possible were Atkinson overly involved.

This willingness to trust others is rooted in some of her sagest advice. In her view, she should "focus only on the things that only I can do." This notion allows her to deal with the distractions that less disciplined leaders may succumb to. As things become more digital, Atkinson is looking to ensure that she can continue to build trust and focus on highest-order areas while her team delivers their responsibilities.

To motivate other people, she works to be "genuine, transparent, and authentic" with her leadership and shows that the organization's strategy is not hers alone. Instead, she makes sure that people know that the Foundation's strategy "is us, not just me" to create deeper buy-in. "Iron sharpens iron," Atkinson shared, to illustrate that being strong and authentic will only strengthen the Foundation's team and results.

Finally, she is making sure that her team has some space and direction enough to pursue time with intentionality. Her thinking is that she and other leaders need to throttle people's time due to the reality that we are (potentially) always-on in the digital day. For Chris Campbell, this throttling is operationalized by a careful attention to calendaring time to think in advance of important discussions and meetings. Atkinson acknowledged that Campbell's approach is an example of "how much technology can be a benefit" if applied with intentionality. As a leader, Atkinson's approach has

(continued)

helped the Foundation weather a pandemic, stand up a new fundraising system, and transition the organization through the retirement and replacement of a beloved University president. While she sometimes deals with overload with brute force and long hours, her "blind trust" tactics and teamwide culture allow her and her team to impressively deliver Oklahoma State's famous orange passion across their entire constituency.

David Nolan, Associate Vice Chancellor, and Travis Soyer, Associate Vice Chancellor, Texas Christian University

Two fundraisers who have thrived despite distraction are Texas Christian University's Travis Soyer and David Nolan. For them, like all of us, dealing with distractions is a daily struggle. In a detailed interview, Chris asked them, with all of the distractions out there, "How do you get anything done?"

Soyer shared: "I'm a zero-inbox type of person. I do not like things going unaddressed (but) I try to tune it out [when I'm out of the office]. I really focus on work when I am in the office." He is focused on "what really needs to get done" to effectively prioritize. He constantly sets a focused direction in his work.

Nolan indicated that TCU has done a lot of work with long-time fundraising counsel Bill McGoldrick, who would emphasize the important-urgent framework to sketch out "the four quadrants and how to map out what goes in what box. Not even thinking about the things in the unimportant and not urgent quadrant ... has been really helpful to clear some of the clutter .... What is important and urgent goes first on the list. In terms of thinking through and categorizing ... this has been really good discipline for me." He also noted that he, too, is a zero-inbox guy, which he feels helps his focus.

The two of them collaborate regularly and align their to-do lists to make sure the operational area under Soyer is in synch with the frontline team that Nolan leads. When summarizing how they try to optimize their work, Nolan summed it up succinctly: "We all want to do more, but we have finite resources. How do we manage those to get the best results? That is where partnership is centered." To that end, Soyer positions himself as the "chief priority setter" for his team to help achieve those results, leading the operational folk down a clear path for their important work.

The net result of the joint focus these two have cultivated is a very organized and aligned team. From handling new requests to managing day-to-day activities, this group delivers results. This in turn has increased trust in a symbiotic partnership.

Joe Manok, Senior Director of Principal Giving, MIT

Joe's story starts out a little differently than most. Joe started his journey working across the street from one of the best universities in the Middle East, American University of Beirut (AUB). A few transitions later and now Joe's office overlooks the Charles River in Cambridge, Massachusetts. Understanding how Joe tackles choices and deals with distractions needs to start on the campus in Lebanon.

The chance to attend college was fortuitous for Joe. In his teens and working across the street from the AUB campus on the Mediterranean Sea, Joe was not aware of scholarships funded by philanthropists. Proximity to campus increased his interactions with professionals at AUB. He was smart and personable enough in his job to be invited to apply at AUB. This was something he had never imagined would be possible. So, when he was accepted and his tuition was covered by a donor's scholarship, two things happened. First, Joe became incredibly focused on maximizing his experiences and he used the combination of his personality and his inherent technical capacity to build and execute a plan to serve and lead at the university. Through the help of a hand-built

(continued)

MS Access database, he was elected the student body president. He served on commissions and advisory boards. He impressed everyone he met, due in part to how hard he worked and how big his vision was, a combination that is not always matched. Second, he committed himself to supporting more beneficiaries of scholarships and advanced education. He was hooked. From that moment, his purpose-driven productivity, what we define as causativity later in the book, was shaped and primed.

When Chris met him, Joe had amassed thousands of Myspace friends, which was notable as it allowed Joe to deal with the potential overload of personal information via technology. Now aware of what "development" was at AUB, he took a position managing operations on the Beirut campus. His mentor and AUB vice president of development, Steve Jeffrey, realized Joe's potential and conscripted him to AUB's New York City offices in a frontline role. From there, Joe quickly developed a prospecting and cultivation approach that blended data with details about personal relationships. He put his knowledge of the Arab world and his multilingual skill set to work. He did so well that MIT (and many others) came calling. He resisted the change due to his loyalty to AUB but eventually agreed to move into his current role at MIT.

Today, Joe continues to be a careful consumer of data to drive his decisions. He keeps a whiteboard of prospects next to his desk. He color-codes those prospects as green (gift given), yellow (gift strategy in motion), or red (gift declined). He keeps the red ones around so he remembers that not every effort results in a gift, but perhaps he can use that relationship to connect MIT elsewhere. He also works hard to view all philanthropy from the same lens. During a recent discussion, Joe shared, "whether that donor is considering a nine-figure gift or a five-figure gift, it is about that person's purpose."

As a fundraiser, Joe has an amazing perspective about donors: he wants interactions with prospective donors to be "as meaningful to the donor as it is to the institution." Over and over, Joe refers to the donor's perspective and the institution's mission. He is merely a (very articulate, strategic, and data-driven) conduit between the two. This allows him to remain very focused. He listens for the prospect's "purpose to see how they might be inspired" to invest.

Interestingly, Joe suggested he feels like he lives in a "quantum state." Like the MIT article on cognitive flexibility and the idea of alternating attention, Joe indicated that he is constantly moving between the data and the people. He is data-driven and personable. He is present and scanning for data points and other connections. His focus comes in part from his ability to achieve flow with his work and to multi-task in ways that are genuine and engaging for his prospects. Joe's experience and approach allow him to deal with the daily distractions and focus on his core purpose. After our discussion with him, Michael observed that Joe has made friends with both distraction and focus.

Cara Giacomini, Vice President of Data, Research, and Technology at the Council for Advancement and Support of Education (CASE)

Cara is a lifelong learner with a PhD in English and Textual Studies. She more recently has been applying her expertise to CASE's positioning and use of data, research, and technology. When we discussed her approach to focusing more on her work, she shared some great, relatable, and repeatable tips.

To start, Giacomini "used to try to be in the 'productivity zone.'" Here she focused on "moving fast on everything but learned that it's a recipe for disaster because eventually you will crash and burn." She found she needed to retrain herself to recognize the value of downtime and how to operate at a sustainable pace. This is a common challenge for many; for instance, Chris felt for years that he needed to keep "the pedal to the metal" as a billing consultant for fear of some unknown future

(continued)

with too little to do and bill. The cost of these approaches can be high and even unhealthy.

For Giacomini, she has attained greater and greater balance in life by focusing on the important things in her work with some useful daily tactics. She journals frequently to zero in on what is happening to and around her. She regularly stretches for 10 minutes or takes a quick neighborhood walk. She also tries to take at least one full day off over the weekend, even if some work needs to be completed. COVID times heightened some of these practices.

Her most effective focus technique is a daily identification of the two most important things to complete each day. The goal is to structure the day to overcome the urgent enough to put time in on these big items. "I want to push something big enough, far enough along each day," Giacomini shared. She uses "focus time" on her calendar (a common tactic we are seeing from a number of professionals) to isolate her efforts. In between times, where she has 15–30 minutes free between meetings, she tries to advance those two items rather than spread work across two dozen details. This has helped her with her productivity, but it is also pretty causative. Because these "big rock" items (explained later in the book) tend to align with the broader purpose of CASE and her key, long-term initiatives, the impact is more profound. Rather than ever getting everything checked off the list (or adopting a zero-inbox approach; she and Chris share the use of the email as searchable databases of sorts), this "big enough, far enough" mantra helps her succeed despite hectic days wrought with distractions.

Your secret sauce for focus may share some of the same themes. Your drive may come from a different place based on your unique circumstances. We have already posited that practices that are best matter more than replicating what others do. And, in Chapter 5, we described the alpha logic, which essentially means that modeling your behavior after the industry's very top performers can do less good than hoped. The important point here is that you take in these ideas and see what applies to your unique skills and situations.

Being Overwhelmed Is the Point, Not the Problem

No matter how good your structure is, it will get overwhelmed. But is that bad? Or is it an opportunity to learn and adjust?

Focused professionals make dozens of choices an hour. Whom to call (back)? Whom to research? What to say? What to write? Which appeal, email, or text to work on next? Which appointment to schedule, cancel, adjust? Layer in meetings, management, travel, and other variables and there is precious little time to gain a foothold on the day. This decision-making requires energy. And that energy is not endless. While hopefully experiences during the COVID-19 pandemic will not be the new normal, remote and hybrid work environments can mean those spinning tops never stop.

In the 1990s, while working at the Saint Louis Zoo, Chris had what he called his "pile of shame." These were all the paper things (email being newish and Google et al. not yet ruling the world) that he would never, ever get to. The weekly *Business Journal* review. Ha! The professional journals and magazine germane to St. Louis businesses and society? No chance! The *Wall Street Journal*? Yeah, right! The pile occupied a big portion of his daily consternation. It created mental load. It was a significant distraction, in part because of all the other work that needed to be done and the potential to do even more impactful things that always seemed just out of reach.

One particularly challenging week, Chris had the benefit of a visit from the Zoo's campaign counsel, Steve Wilkerson of Pierpont Wilkerson. Mr. Wilkerson was exceptionally good at his craft and Chris wanted to soak up what he could, but the piles of work beckoned. During this onsite visit, Mr. Wilkerson invited Chris to dinner to talk through prospects and campaign strategy. It was a kind and intellectually exciting offer, but one Chris declined because, right next to that pile of shame was a pile of checks that needed validation for receipting. Seeing this as a problem, Chris complained that there were too many gifts to finish processing. Mr. Wilkerson's retort was searingly elegant: "Having too many gifts is not a problem, it is the point!" And, with that, the two headed off to dinner.

Too Much of a Good Thing

A structure that buckles under success is not a bad structure. It is worthy of inspection. Success is a good problem to have. Such is the fate of every aspiring and motivated fundraiser. If you're succeeding, you have too many calls, too many emails, too many texts, too many meetings, and too many prospects and donors. To-do lists stretch on and on. We also often give too little staffing, budget, and resources in order to meet that unhealthy fixation on overhead costs. Unplanned visits and conversations run (or sometimes ruin) the week. And, ideally, gift- and stewardship-related correspondence poses a recurring threat to one's ability to leave their desk on time. Those gifts are the point. It is the fundraiser's job to engage so many so well that the volume of response is overwhelming. It is the job of the marketing colleague to drive too many eyeballs to count toward organizational messaging and, ideally, calls to action. It is the job of effective prospect development professionals to bring more prospects for discovery than can be covered in years, much less weeks and months.

A central message in focused fundraising is that the *potential* for being overwhelmed is indeed the point. The missions that need serving are missions that can feel overwhelming. The prospective prospect base should be sizable. The areas and recognition opportunities for support should be so voluminous as to be hard to remember. Ideally, data points are well enough maintained and technology well enough aligned to establish sophisticated email and direct response efforts that raise engagement and dollars. The trick for focused fundraisers is knowing how to set a focused direction. The lessons are in how to acknowledge the potential for being overwhelmed while avoiding spinning in place.

Great insight here comes from the professional sports world. Elite athletes have generally established an ability to focus at greater levels than others. Daniel Kahneman's *Thinking, Fast and Slow* explains the phenomenon in terms of System 1, or reactive thinking, and System 2, slow thinking. Less experienced and talented players tend toward reactive approaches. However, those who spend more time learning, often slowly and incrementally over long periods of time, can bring to bear their studies in System 2 learning to improve their ability to handle overwhelming stimuli when System 1 sets in. So, when the ball is snapped and an elite quarterback has seconds to make a decision before being pummeled, the ability to focus is essential.

The very best fundraisers possess a similar superpower to paradoxically speed up results by seeming to slow things down. With potentially overwhelming distractions swirling around them and their constituents, they manage to listen and engage, drawing prospects closer to the organization's mission in the process. Being overwhelmed is welcomed, in that way. Having so many great prospects and donors to engage is an exciting challenge. They RAISE the topics that matter most, and they make a habit out of refining their work.

Deriving what matters most is a key component of dealing with overwhelming situations. As Blaire Atkinson from the Oklahoma State University Foundation shared, you will benefit from the mantra "Do only what only I can do." As the saying goes, you want avoid being a jack-of-all-trades, but a master of none. Such situations also call to mind the Serenity Prayer, whereby one is reminded to focus on what they can control and accept the things they cannot. These pieces of advice, when gathered together, prove to be helpful guidance in addressing overwhelming situations. This was Art Ochoa's advice: three things will get you promoted and three things might get you fired; the rest you should try to ignore.

A new vice chancellor for advancement demonstrated focus to Chris while strolling together on campus. Chris knew the VC was absorbing a mountain of data, reports, and details. For instance, his new team's practice was to have well over 150 prospects assigned per portfolio (which Gladwell's *Tipping Point* and related studies show to be, well, beyond the tipping point on what an individual can handle; see Chapter 7 for details). While strolling along the quad, a colleague shouted to the new VC: "Hey there. Hope you are settling in well." The VC offered a sincere hello and thanks in return. Chris was impressed. "How have you had time to get to know folks so far?" To which the VC flatly stated: "I have no idea who that was ... I have about 40 Board members, 15 deans, and 20 families that give us millions of dollars ... honestly, those are the only people I've had time to consider so far." His bluntness is a reminder for all of us: focus often involves tough trade-offs.

In this case, being overwhelmed was not an option. There was no forced focus; just the natural focus of wanting to excel. As much as the Golden Rule—"do unto others as you would have others do unto you"—makes the world a better place, in an overwhelming fundraising world, another golden rule—"those who have the gold make the rules"—can sometimes simplify your options for better or worse. Tough trade-offs are often a part of focus. And with that clarity comes the ability to structure your work. You can treat all fairly and with respect. And when your structures buckle, you can remember that being overwhelmed is the point, not the problem.

We have now covered structure, the fourth ingredient to setting focused direction. Let's turn to the fifth and final part: evolving your approach.

12

Evolve Your Approach

To EVOLVE YOUR approach means to learn from your experience. In this last section of the RAISE framework, we encourage you to engage what Carol Dweck called a "growth mindset."

A growth mindset begins with humility. Humility often starts with asking what appear to be dumb questions. In James Ryan's best-selling book *Wait, What?*, the subject is how to ask powerful questions, some of which certainly feel dumb. As we learn from Ryan, oddly enough, there may be no more powerful questions than "Huh?" or "Come again?" Essentially, if we could boil down all the neuroscience and focus articles and books we have read, it would simply enjoin us to ask these most basic questions on a more regular basis. We all ought to be suspicious of what we think we know. And just like the book *Wait, What?* illustrates, powerful questions are powerful because they are directional.

Yes, directional. A good, powerful question can stop us in our tracks, or it can get us going in a direction we never thought possible. If you want to routinely set focused direction, it's best to get in the habit of checking what you think you heard. Michael remembers vividly one of the most powerful questions he was ever asked. In response, he didn't ask "Wait, what?" verbally, but his response was

107

essentially the same thing. Michael had been talking to a mentor about figuring out his career direction. Twenty minutes into Michael's meandering explanation of the difficulties of figuring it out, this particular mentor, who had a somewhat deadpan way of talking, just looked at Michael as if to say "Huh?" Then, after a lengthy pause he asked in a slow, but direct and interested tone: "How do you know *this* isn't the process of figuring it out?"

"Wait, what?" Just like that, a whole gnawing existential problem seemed to evaporate.

Where Are We Now?

What's the happiest ending for a meeting? In our opinion, it's when everyone in the meeting is grateful for the time, feels good about the resolution, and voluntarily offers up what they are going to do before the next meeting. "Great meeting. I'll contact Steve." "I'll write the proposal." And so on.

When you create room for this kind of closure, you can consistently evolve your approach. If you're the leader, you can ask: "So, where are we now?" Asking this with enough time left in the meeting can surface new insights and actions. Alternatively, if you're an attendee, you can simply jump in: "Can I tell you where I think we are?" Then, there's plenty of room for everyone to share their POV and perhaps propose what they'll do.

So, this final stage to set focused direction is to ask a powerful question: "Where are we now?" We think of this as strategic centering. You center on where the group is. Done frequently, you stay iterative and continuously evolving. Often this question just brings together the ideas that floated up from prior discussions or experiences. Although it feels risky perhaps to not close a meeting with a forward-looking question like what our next steps are, keep in mind that we are wired to be forward-looking. The challenge is that the tech tug and growth culture tend to be action-first rather than focus-first, so it feels risky to not *always* put the future first. Often the next steps come up naturally when we leave room for them.

Evolving your approach is worthwhile, of course, but like anything worthwhile it is easier said than done. To borrow a phrase from Fred

Kofman, author of *Conscious Business*, it may be common sense but it is not common practice. Evolving your approach will make you exemplary. It can also make work a lot more interesting and innovative.

Evolving the Pyramid

Is it possible to evolve your approach on any topic? We think it is. In this section we put RAISE to the test on a hallmark of fundraising: the giving pyramid. Let's RAISE this topic together.

The giving pyramid—the assumption that giving is wider at the low-dollar base than the high-dollar peak—is one of our industry's more significant *potential* distractions. This well-meaning approach to campaign and strategic planning has one major flaw: it is almost always wrong. Chris has seen hundreds of such pyramids over the past few decades at nonprofits large and small. From this experience, no matter how much time is spent with the data and no matter how carefully analyses are done, most pyramids these days look more like an hourglass, or a flagpole, or something other than what the industry has been conveying for decades. Entire wings of fundraising consulting have been based on building the pyramid, only to yield a stale, formulaic approach. For comprehensive campaigns, the base is often teeming with generous donors who came nowhere near their prescribed capacity. Over-the-transom donors often constitute substantial portions of campaign results. In a recently completed campaign analysis, Chris found that around one-third of the organization's best donors were unknown, performed well beyond their rated capacity, or had no rating at all. Does this make the prospecting and analytics work obsolete? No. Are scoring and optimizing pools and portfolios a waste of time? Far from it. But to make "the pyramid" matter requires a focused fundraiser to rethink—to evolve the approach. Despite the shaky evidence for its accuracy, the idea of caring about all levels of giving—that a few donors will be atop the list of most generous but that too narrow a base will risk future campaigns—is much more important than the practical utility of a pyramid that never seems to match predictions.

Now let's put RAISE to this tried-although-typically-not-true gift pyramid for campaigns.

- **Recognize your POV.** Namely, ask yourself who wants a giving pyramid. Who are they? The Board? A consulting firm? Consider who the "we" are in this situation. Is it you and your leadership? Is it volunteers? Then consider "it." Where did the giving pyramid come from? Why do you believe giving pyramids are useful expressions of campaign strategy? Finally, consider your own point of view. Ask yourself if using the pyramid helps your work. Are you better off thinking this way? Does it dissuade you from seeking even bigger gifts because you already have that $xx million gift in hand at a certain level? Hopefully not, but it can.

- **Assess your standards.** What standards apply? How do you know you will have a good giving pyramid? What is it about your organization and campaign that may make the pyramid useful? Are there better ways to reflect both your organization's past results and your future potential? What does the pyramid do for your Board? Your culture and your level of urgency? Your donor stewardship? How about ratings standards and practices; are those solid? You may find that the pyramid has some unintended consequences, such as perhaps dissuading a Board member from giving a bigger gift when they see a more comfortable spot among the voluminous lower-level gifts "needed" for the campaign.

- **Inspire your efforts.** What makes a pyramid worthwhile? Does a pyramid reflect your organization's value and mission? If you were Stanford, perhaps the pyramid's resemblance to your cardinal is apropos, but for many there are much more brand-oriented ways to convey this data. Can you get creative? Most pyramids, for instance, leave out corporate and foundation details because these entities are typically not researched and capacity-scored in the same way individual prospects are. Leaving out organization giving and the outcomes from over-the-transom results can miss out on 50% or more of a campaign outcome; what good is the pyramid in that case?

- **Structure your work.** What structures support what you're trying to do? Ask yourself if the data that make up such reporting are real(istic). Are the codes and values trustworthy? Screening data can be directional, but it is sometimes not accurate. Too often, the numbers we hope for have no basis in results and wealth indicators are missing liabilities in the calculation of capacity. You will never know prospects' net worth; even *Forbes* calculations are estimates. In a recent case, for instance, Chris found a client's $1 billion-plus campaign had over 30% of the total raised from prospects/donors who were not scored in the prospect pool and hence not in the "pyramid." What good is that? This pyramid is starting to look less like the majestic Stanford cardinal and more like Charlie Brown's Christmas tree.

- **Evolve your approach.** Where are you now? At UCLA in the early 2010s, an enterprising research analytics professional came up with an amazing visual to replace the stale pyramid: a river. This river was filled with fish and other creatures of all sizes (and values to the person fishing). Some were deep in the middle of the river (cold and unlikely). Some were small but right at the surface, next to the fisher and seemingly easy to catch. Some creatures made less sense to catch and so were distractions. And, all along the way, the river is moving, refreshing the waters below, representing the changing environment and allowing in new fish (aka prospects) for consideration. Now, this river metaphor may capture campaign readiness vis-à-vis your prospect pool better than a stale pyramid. It is also worth noting that the technology we have to identify, track, analyze, and report out on prospect pools allows for incredible innovation. Hopefully, your team is at least able to use the sophisticated side of MS Excel pivot tables, but ideally you have data visualization and analytics in place to test out and evolve new ways to examine prospects than that often-wrong pyramid.

So, did we talk you out of using a gift pyramid for your next campaign? We doubt it. But did we help you isolate some aspects about what you have done or plan to do that will cut through the noise? Get you better positioned and focused? Will you better tackle foundation and corporate prospects in your planning? Will you consider how your audience thinks about what you show them and perhaps make it more meaningful? Will you try to close the loop on those "unrated" prospects and over-the-transom donors whose contributions might make up a big chunk of the campaign result, leaving little analytical value in their wake? We hope so. Much of *Focused Fundraising* is not just about behavior changes and categorical decisions. It is also about shifts in perspective. Incremental shifts add up over time. Remember that a construct like the gift pyramid, for all its faults, can help you zero in on important areas, gaps, trends, and patterns that need explanation. As you evolve your approach you are gaining focus.

Balancing between meaning and myth, real and really neat, are all so tricky because visuals, anecdotes, and analogies are so sticky. To learn how to evolve, we now explore how to further evaluate your circumstances.

Angry Donor Policies: The Problem with Stories

Just as environmental groups inspire us to "think global and act local," focus requires something similar. Focus means that we "think systems and tell stories." Despite the urgency and allure of the abnormal and anomalous, you need systems to evolve, not be based on risk aversion or one-off situations. It's vital to ask where you are now, so you can put the whole process in context. Without situating yourself in the current state, even the most focused fundraisers can come unglued at the sight of an anecdotal issue. Even if you think systems and tell stories, sometimes the stories overwhelm the systems.

Here is the scene: a donor's event invite gets lost. Time passes. Then one day the donor calls to complain that they did not get invited to the event. An engagement officer fields the complaint. Now, *Oh no!*, the system is broken! The sky is falling! The organization's fundraising and events will never be the same. Bulwarks are devised to ensure that said error never manifests again. Time is spent in looking for and avoiding these errors, because ultimately, we are hoping to diminish future risks, in the form of fewer phone calls from angry donors.

As we discussed earlier, our brains are wired to recall exceptions and problems; we are built to remember painful moments so we can avoid them in the future. Unless one guards against this tendency, it makes sense, really, that systemically oriented, inefficient, or ineffective policies and procedures get drafted. "None shall pass!" is the rally cry of the gift team for fear of mistakes. Reports have new data for fear of misinterpretation. Triple checks are added to double checks. During these moments, a focused fundraiser can be persuaded to lose focus, to zero in on these details, exceptions, and errors, and to accept risk aversion as a starting point.

The two primary products of risk aversion in fundraising are "angry donor policies" and "triple-checked processes." These do not evolve your approach; they often cripple it. Neither work very well. Mistakes can and will continue to happen, and in the meantime these "solutions" become much more costly than the problem. Nowhere is this more clear than in gift administration, explained in detail later in the book.

To assuage donors disappointed with errors, nonprofits have a tendency to adopt elaborate traps to avoid the same fate in the future. These do not always fail, but they do not tend to succeed. Volume is generally too high, time too short, and speed too fast to avoid the occasional issue. Too often, we see the shop decide to add a code to every gift and pledge for eternity to indicate something that happens 0.01% of the time. We see tribute recognition policies result in processes that are three or four times slower because they are trying to ensure that every letter is always correct. To avoid risk, they incur opportunity cost as fundraisers get caught up in minutiae.

Internally, many fundraisers are heaped with added work around "triple-checking." Just one more check is supposed to avoid the dreaded errors that prompted the angry donor policy in the first place. We do not have time to call donors to thank them because we are reviewing a batch of gifts seeking the tiniest of errors. Fundraisers "need to see" those pledge reminders because of that one time when Jane received the wrong balance. Trust in data across the organization diminishes, leading to wasted time redoing others' work. To avoid risk, you further distract your team's attention with low-return labor.

Later in the book, we examine the importance of a "front of the line" mentality for the organization's most treasured donors. At the top of the pyramid, all bets are off and all stops should be pulled out. The risk aversion here that leads to angry donor policies that will not work and time-consuming reviews that should yield few results is a real threat to a fundraiser's focus.

So, what can you do instead? Evolve your approach. Ask: So where are we now? What have we learned? Perhaps RAISE it as a topic. And of course you can always try these five words: "Okay. We will fix it." Then fix it. If there is a systemic database-level problem, really resolve it and train the team in the improved process that avoids such errors. If it was truly anecdotal, apologize. Say "Yes … and" as in, "Yes, that was a terrible mistake, and we will try to avoid it in the future." Do not give in to the tendency to build a more elaborate process or more particular policies for one-off situations. Policy by exception is no policy at all.

Finally, have some grace in the process. Nonprofit work can mean life or death. It is critically important. It deserves everyone's focus. It can also never be perfect. The time it takes to drill into an error is often not worth the distraction from one's primary purpose. No one would encourage such erroneous outcomes, but understanding them and changing your response to them will move your team to a whole new level of potential.

■　■　■

You have now completed the RAISE framework. In the toolkit at the end of the book you will find further applications of RAISE as well as coaching prompts. We encourage you to test out the self-coaching prompts as well as the team prompts. To RAISE a topic is to elevate your focus without forcing it. You have gone through each of the five phases to set a focused direction. The remainder of *Focused Fundraising* is about taking this understanding to your organization. Because organizational life begins with culture, we start there. And now that we have discussed evolving your personal approach, culture is a great area to adopt a growth mindset. There can be no real evolution without cultural change.

PART

III

Focused Fundraising Teams

Culture eats strategy for breakfast.

—Peter Drucker

A FITTING-IF-BRIEF SUMMATION of the thesis of *Focused Fundraising* can be found in Peter Drucker's observation about culture and strategy above. A similar and funnier sentiment is ne'er-do-well Mike Tyson's "Everybody has a plan until they get punched in the face." Every ding, buzz, and flash is an assault on the senses. Every exception and error can lead to dizzying distractions. Each distraction diminishes our larger achievements. Cultivating a focused fundraising organization requires everyone's buy-in and support. You can lead by example.

As a leader or team member, when you adopt a focus-first mentality, you begin to handle yours' and others' needs differently. You are perceived as more intentional and more present. And when you apply RAISE to topics you're facing, you further reinforce a calm, centered focus. With good self-care and regular practice, the 4 Ms, the tech tug, and instant overload do not preoccupy your attention. Focus becomes a natural part of your day, no force necessary.

To bring this level of focus to those around you, the remainder of *Focused Fundraising* goes further into the organizational aspects of fundraising. In this section, you will read about familiar challenges. What teams do not have too many things in progress? Who does not struggle with extra steps in gift processing? Who already has all of the governance and change management their team needs? With RAISE in mind, you can take a fresh look at your team and set a focused direction.

13

The Importance of Culture

DOES YOUR ORGANIZATION acknowledge the need for focus? Does your organization put focus first or action first? Honest reflection on these types of questions can start you thinking about team culture. Reflecting on culture is important because the best-laid plans require more than reading a book, writing a strategic plan, creating a gift pyramid, or establishing policies and procedures manuals. Edicts from consultants only go so far. Best practices from other organizations rarely fit. Great teams—focused teams—live their strategies because of their culture. They exude confidence in their purpose. They are excited to tackle challenges. They have a shared culture that acknowledges the need for focus in the constant craziness of nonprofit life.

Bringing RAISE to your team requires a twofold plan. First, decide how you personally will apply what you have learned. You can begin by applying RAISE to the very topic or going deeper with the coaching prompts and discussion questions in the toolkit. Second, determine how your organization will apply the approaches and lessons in this book. Starting with culture and then creating a change-friendly environment are vital steps in turning your team into a focused fundraising team.

"Culture" is loaded with meaning, nuance, and potential misunderstanding. Political culture, ethnic culture, and other aspects of culture dominate the academic literature. It is Peter Drucker's notion that "culture eats strategy for breakfast," though that is vital here. The central idea is that a shared set of values about focused direction establishes norms. If the strategy is too far afield from the organization's reality, it will fail; hence "culture eats strategy."

Culture and Change Management

Culture, of course, is not monolithic or immutable. Organizational culture is defined by subcultures. As team members, processes, tools, policies, and leadership change, so can culture. It evolves. Managing these changes becomes a critical consideration for focused fundraising shops. Change management is well-defined in the body of literature for organizational improvement. From John Kotter to Spencer Johnson's simple but elegant *Who Moved My Cheese?* to the more detailed directives in Dan and Chip Heath's *Switch*, there are plenty of great books and explanations of change management. What is important here—and to capitalize on the direction of focused fundraising—is how change management can be used to establish focus-friendly conditions. How can you enable a culture that diminishes distractions and overload, tames the tech tug, corrals the 4 Ms, and normalizes focused direction?

In your own life, you can take the understanding in *Focused Fundraising* and apply it to your own personal practices. To tune into your own preferences, you can RAISE the topic of reducing distractions. For example, one focused fundraiser adopted the following set of personal guidelines:

Turn off notifications, but allow family members' in. Stop looking at email without a purpose. Before checking, ask: Do I have time to process what I read? Am I looking for a particular update? Curate news and information feeds. Well-crafted aggregations of headlines in one spot beat tooling all over the internet at random times for information. In the office, create RSS feeds and alerts about key constituents. Choose Facebook comment feeds wisely!

At the team level, change and culture can be much more difficult to influence. For instance, if the team RAISEs the topic of insufficient reports, how does the culture relate to it? The team may start to shift from thinking about reports as one-dimensional, often archaic, and inefficient printed pieces of paper to considering them as data visualization for decision-making. With the shift in perspective, the chances for focused direction on reporting go up. But what about historical practices? Do you need that 8½×11 PDF report? Printed out? In a binder? Probably not. But do you need new definitions and a common language? Definitely!

Readiness is a major factor in culture change. For example, if the team RAISEs the topic of slow IT projects, the temptation is to adopt something like Agile, a proven software development philosophy. But is your team ready for it? Is your culture ready for it? Well, that depends. The incremental and iterative nature of the approach can lead to limited and myopic recapitulations of yesterday's systems. This is a clear case of form NOT following function, whereby subject matter experts are given very little time to think about very small parts of the big picture. The result of an overeager embrace of Agile can be what Zuri Group's Brandon Ferris coined a Legacy 2.0 system, which is where the team just recreates their old database in shinier packaging. If an organization simply re-creates what they have always done, they can expect only meager improvements despite spending potentially millions of dollars and thousands of hours. By calling this out and helping organizations actually improve how they do their work in designing their new technology ecosystem, Ferris has become one of the best CRM implementation consultants on the planet. The willingness to take Ferris's advice, though, often comes down to culture and readiness. Readiness comes from understanding what the change means from the spinning top—people, process, reporting, data, and technology— as well as considering environmental factors.

With the pandemic upending the current work-life paradigm in the United States, this issue is particularly salient: **Presence does not equal productivity**. Culture drives results.

My only real motivation is not to be hassled; that, and the fear of losing my job. But you know, Bob, that will only make someone work just hard enough not to get fired.

—Peter Gibbons, in the motion picture *Office Space*

Teams like Peter's may survive, but not for long. Focused fundraising shops will do their best to avoid chasms between morale and purpose. Purpose-driven shops will make more headway in staff retention and in results.

Improvements at the individual and organizational level can help us move closer to the ideals established by Drucker and help us avoid the more recent traps detailed in Cal Newport's *Deep Work*. Specifically, Newport highlights the dangers of the always-on, hard-to-focus, "second shift" that many of us do. The tech tug can steal from you and from your team. Who drives a 24/7 culture? Do team members feel guilty about the need to decompress, or is this need recognized?

Sensitivity to culture is vital. Stakeholders need to understand the benefits of change. They need to buy in. Everyone needs to know the "what's in it for me" (WIIFM), because digital content providers have created a countervailing force that is telling your brain something different. That is, Instagram, Twitter, and TikTok are telling your brain to focus not on your purpose but instead on their content. Controlling the tech tug, rather than being controlled by it, requires a strong sense of purpose. To maximize our impact and achieve greater focus, we need to evolve our organizational cultures and our personal approaches. There are tools to help like the Focused Fundraising Maturity Model, which we describe later.

Authenticity Is Vital to Evolve

Culture is most vibrant when it allows for differences. Focused fundraisers can take all shapes and sizes. From analytically oriented data sifters to Rolodex-loving paper printers, it is hard to say there is a "type" that is more productive than not. One of the leading fundraising consultancies coined a common theme around fundraising being part

art and part science. Most of us live on this continuum between being pretty artfully focused on people to pretty cleverly focused on data. Being yourself along that continuum is essential. To repeat: being who you are in the balance between art and science is critical because it reflects your authenticity. Examining these two variants is a useful way to think about how a fundraiser's authentic style affects focus and culture.

A Tale of Two Fundraisers: The Artist and the Scientist

Focused fundraisers share some characteristics. They tend to heavily emphasize donor experience and align donors' life goals with how their organizations can improve communities and the world. They tend to understand that charitable giving is a team sport and that the donor's stewardship is vitally important to success. They believe in the mission and, as a result, tend to remain with their institutions for much, much longer than the fairly abysmal national averages suggest. Penelope Burke's analysis showed in 2016 that 50% of fundraisers in 2,700 surveyed planned to stay in their role less than two years. The most common reason was burnout. Imagine what it must be today! Focused fundraisers like Art Ochoa, who has spent about two decades at Cedars-Sinai, buck this trend.

While principles and outcomes are generally similar across great fundraising professionals, styles often vary substantially. The range of styles can be summed up along the continuum of "art" and "science." Artists feel and listen and create. Scientists study and analyze and test. Of course, one can do both and blend them throughout, yet the archetypal artist fundraiser will tend toward relationships and the science-oriented gift officer will lean more heavily on data.

One way that focused fundraisers evolve their approach is by identifying their place on the continuum between art and science, dedicating themselves to their craft, *and* teaming with colleagues who complement their skills. The art and science can be applied at the organizational level, too.

One dynamic fundraising duo along this continuum stands out during Chris's practitioner career: Cynthia Holter and Jeff Huntington. Cynthia is the senior vice president at the Saint Louis Zoo. Jeff is her right hand and partner as the Zoo's director of development. They are very much alike in donor centrism, thoughtfulness about donor stewardship, and dedication to the institutional mission. The progress they have made over a few decades is as impressive as any organization's like it. Huge capital efforts, deeply effective community campaigns, corporate responsibility initiatives, and endowed funds sprung from this duo's hard work. Of course, they would say it is all about the donors and their colleagues and the animals and the environment. And they are right. Yet the tale here is that, despite their individual strengths, they are even more potent together.

Cynthia started her career in the late 1980s. Smart, brave, and personable, she managed university campaigning for a land-grant university and she flourished. What stood out to most was her attention and presence. She had—and has—an ability to be present in discussions, listen, learn, store tidbits away about people's lives, and send the most thoughtful notes months later, all while building a detailed strategy for engagement. The artist at work would read the room, connect the people, and make certain the mission of the institution was front and center. Her superpower was in understanding donors and helping them achieve their goals.

Jeff is equally talented and passionate. When he joined the Zoo from a smaller nonprofit, his thoroughness was obvious and critically important to his impact. While not a technologist at heart, he sought data and connections; his superpowers included a willingness to take risks and learn from them in a formal way. He was persistent in seeking more and better ways to engage prospects in the community. He was studious. He was connecting membership, sponsorship, event, and major giving efforts to maximize outcomes. His careful approach was scientific in the ways he would test approaches, never tiring from the effort.

Reading this, you likely see yourself in both of these fine fundraisers. Both have strengths. Both lead efforts to raise more and more money for a worthy cause. And both share traits. Cynthia was surely strategic and Jeff was always engaging. The secret sauce here, and in many shops, was the combination of their superpowers. They shared in strategy, work, and results in ways that leveraged both of their talents, as a team. This complementary combination is one of the many lessons in achieving focused fundraising.

The Unfocused Fundraiser: A Cautionary Tale

"Unfocused" could simply mean "distracted." In a bigger sense, though, "unfocused" points to something more damaging than looking at your iPhone, multi-tasking during a Zoom call, or tuning out your partner while you watch YouTube. An "unfocused fundraiser" is missing the point, wasting their time, and sometimes inadvertently sabotaging the very organization they are intending to advance.

How can this be? How could someone fundraising in an unfocused way hurt your culture and actually make things worse? Think for a moment about hiking in the woods. You come across a three-way split and need to make a choice: left, forward, or right. Which option you choose depends mightily on how you arrived at that spot. How much do you know about where you want to wind up? And why did you start on the hike in the first place? There are so many variables. Do you have a map? Do you have a targeted destination? What time box are you working with?

Without purpose and goals as guideposts, one can just as easily get lost at work. A focused hiker would make choices around purpose and knowledge, such as which direction the trails head in or which option is going uphill or downhill. The same should be the case for a focused fundraiser. When presented with choice, the professional asks, "Which path likely leads to the best engagement or gift?" or "Which option best supports our mission?" Focus saves tremendous time from dead ends and sidetracks. How much time can be wasted on events that are abandoned or have little impact? How about time spent on prospects that are unlikely to ever pan out? Or on projects that do not happen? So, while styles will vary along the art–science continuum, it is imperative that the focused fundraiser remains, well, focused. Just as an unmoored hiker might make an uninformed choice that substantially diminishes their enjoyment, an unmoored fundraiser may go "down the rabbit hole" in ways that do not achieve much more than perhaps the appearance of productivity. A focused fundraiser, and focused fundraising culture, values results more than activity.

14

Prospect Development

DEVELOPING A FOCUSED fundraising team means bringing focus to every aspect of the work. In this chapter we explore some of the basic building blocks for prospect development—a prospect list, an initial visit, and a virtual visit—as elemental to focused fundraising. In their most basic sense, fundraising results follow from developing some kind of prospect list, and then working the list in a way that is mindful and strategic. There can be great sophistication to determining who is on the list, why, and how the list is "worked."

The world of a fundraiser can be exceedingly complicated. For those readers who have explored game theory, think of every prospective donor as a multi-iteration actor whose own choices and preferences are hard to know. Add to the complexity the needs and expectations of bosses and boards, and one can quickly see how challenging the work can be. With increasing noise, distraction, and choice added to the equation, the difficulty of making the right choices becomes clear.

On the other hand, despite the complexity, focused fundraising work has some elemental components. Focused shops align their institution's mission with the interests of their donors. Donors don't generally get tricked into giving their gifts. These shops communicate with and cultivate prospective donors so that the impact of one's engagement is clear. They celebrate the positive impact they have on their communities. These are big-ticket items.

For day-to-day work, a fundraiser can establish great focus by zeroing in on the fundamentals of prospect development. Great prospecting need not be complex. There should be a pool of prospective donors, qualification and cultivation approaches, strategic solicitations, and meaningful stewardship. With the distractions of the day, these simple (but not simplistic) elements can be overlooked in favor of fancier efforts. However, the focused fundraiser will realize quickly that concentrating on the fundamentals is more important.

Let's turn to a detailed evaluation of these fundraiser-specific fundamentals. Getting these components organized and under control will aid focus as much as any more complex steps. This section is for the individual fundraiser whose organization is seeking to strip away the noise and make better choices.

Prospect List

So, what is the starting point for being a fundraiser and being a fundraising organization? It is having prospects from whom you are seeking investments in your organization's mission. As a result, your prospect list is the single most important front-end aspect of your work as a fundraiser. (Your donor list is your most important back-end aspect.) And, for too many of you, that prospect list is a hot mess!

The organizational-level guidance on focusing these lists can include delving into pools with machine learning and other tools. Great lists created according to agreed-upon practices and governed by shared policy are essential raw materials. These help you answer the question: What should you do (today!) with your list, knowing what you know now? Check out the following four points to focus your prospect list.

1. **Despite how fast things are moving and how many choices you have, seek out prospects who make the most sense to engage.** Data points in your prospect system can tell you which prospects to focus on, when, and why. But remember the context per prospect on your list. These are items that often do not get coded into a

database and are hard to analyze, but will make or break your cultivation efforts. As much as you are hoping to make choices efficiently and effectively, you are doing so against the backdrop of the typically unknown thinking of your dance partner; that is, most of your prospects are pretty close to a black box in terms of decision-making, at least at the early stages of the relationship.

2. **Keep your list manageable.** There is substantial social science work on the seemingly natural breaking point of 150 relationships in community building and interpersonal understanding. The trend in fundraising is to have lists even smaller than 150 assignments. Some organizations are espousing a 25-prospect list, but largely ignoring the cultivation and stewardship prospects that need your attention. If you have a larger list, or if your list has unknown names with questionable capacity and inclination details, cull it. Do it today. Jettison those prospects that make your list unwieldy and distract you. If your team's policies and practices will not support this move, copy this page and send it to your boss's boss. Seriously, right-sizing your prospect list is a sure way to gain focus.

3. **Include your "why" to maximize philanthropic giving to your institution.** When we look at portfolios, sometimes your "why" seems to need reiterating. If your list includes never-donors because they were on a national list of, say, young presidents, you may not have the right focus. Refine your list to those whose likely "why" will align with your organization's mission and your specific role. This may mean reassigning prospects that actually are better suited for a colleague's portfolio. It might require you to "quit" on a prospect assignment. Remember, though, that quitting can help you focus. This is like the power of saying no, or at least yes, and .... Using your "why" for when to quit (as well as giving it the 3×3×3 approach shown in Figure 14.1) will make decisions clearer and easier. Scale your efforts according to the expected capacity and giving levels of your prospects. Not sure if a prospect can make a major gift? Cut them loose after three tries. Convinced a prospect has principal giving-level potential? Don't let go until you have tried three times more than you would with a major gift prospect, including trying some truly creative efforts along the way.

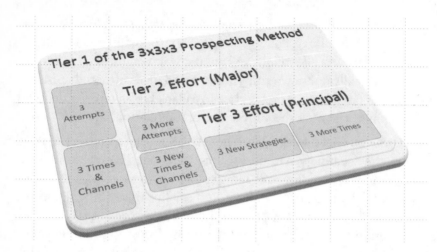

Figure 14.1 Applying the 3×3×3 approach to determine how much more to focus on a prospect

4. **Remember that your technology options may be changing how you work and think, and not always for the better.** Distraction can be beneficial in some ways, but being distracted too often and in the wrong settings can damage your results. Keep your phone on silent, with only favorited contacts allowed to make your phone make noise. Turn off every alert you can. Trust us, you will still look at your phone plenty. Recall that Chris picks up his phone on average 86 times a day and only his wife's and kids' texts or phone calls actually make a noise. Beyond your email and personal devices, cool new solutions can be appealing and appalling. It is important for you to be vigilant for incongruous context around those areas that analytics and cool tools might miss. That prospect you have never heard of scored great on that screening? Great, but make sure the real estate attributed to that scoring is, well, real. Your new AI-driven application is telling you to contact someone next due to, say, gift timing guidance? Great, but look at the record first and make sure that call is timely based on other variables such as solicitation plans, family issues, or third-party giving.

Your prospect list is a first line of defense in dealing with digital distractions. Once you have these under control, you have a chance to think more deeply about how to engage those prospects on the list, starting with getting an initial visit.

Getting the Initial Visit

A prospect is not much of a prospect if they will not agree to visit with you. Ever. There are tales of lore about the over-the-transom big gift someone provided with no prompting ever, but these are exceptions among the exceptional. For those with portfolios, visiting with someone, in person or digitally, is the likeliest path to realizing your fundraising goals. Prospect visits are typically the leading indicator of future major giving. So, how can you focus to make the visit happen?

For starters, think about the visit from the prospect's perspective. They are likely struggling with distraction and overwhelming choices, too. No offense, but why would they spend their finite time with you? Figuring this out is essential. Too often, our pleas and ploys to get a visit start with "I will be in town ...," "The dean would love to meet with you ...," or "Doctor Jane's research is vitally important ...," rather than a strategy to leverage that prospective donor's situation and needs. Getting focused on the prospect will provide much better results than angling your pitch.

With the prospect in mind, turn your attention to your own focus. Can you find 10–15 minutes to RAISE the topic of this donor? If not, are they even worth your time? This is not intended to be prep work just before meeting. Instead, this is the sort of real thinking that Cal Newton's *Deep Work* suggests. You can get to this work if you value it, or find a coworker to make it more fun. You can gather everything you know about the prospect. You can review available research. You can look into the database, paying close attention to any past behavior such as giving, event attendance, volunteerism, and velocity of the relationship. You can do a little (very little, really) googling. And, once you have these details in mind, RAISE the topic. Why would they visit with you? What would make it a good visit for them? What might inspire them? The desire to have more information should not imply time-consuming research, just the essentials. The thought work is what matters.

Once you think it through, a focused direction usually emerges. If you believe their past giving could grow substantially with involvement by leadership, push for that. If you believe the prospect is not very likely to visit, much less give enough to warrant a visit, consider putting them into a more automated channel. Balance these ideas against the potential gain. You are now conducting the same risk assessment around utility and distraction that our brains were designed to deliver millennia ago. What is your "why?," what is their "why?," and can you get them to intersect?

Most of this advice is offered with the expectation that an in-person visit will be your main priority. Fundraiser after fundraiser tends to proclaim the primacy of the in-person visit. Many fundraising managers seem to agree. Yet, these days, that preference and reality have changed, leading you to determine how to leverage the virtual visit. While the jury may be out on the future of digital-driven engagement in lieu of in-person visits, the dilemma is less stark than it once was: some of your prospects will prefer virtual visits. As Brent Grinna, founder and CEO of EverTrue, has found in his company's research, the "some" that prefer this type of engagement is growing and worth your time. His team has built some cool tools to help with digital engagement and virtual visits, explained next. Grinna shared the following when he discussed his approach to the initial visit:

Beginning just before the start of the Covid-19 pandemic, EverTrue helped create more than two dozen Donor Experience programs at colleges across the country. In these programs, fundraisers (called DXOs) use EverTrue technology to manage 1,000-person portfolios. They rely solely on virtual visits and remote engagement to connect with their assigned prospects.

In analyzing thousands of virtual donor visits made by DXO teams in FY21, EverTrue discovered that it takes an average of 6.6 touchpoints to secure a visit. That means polite persistence is key to booking that Zoom conversation. Mindfulness before every email or video message is critical to capturing that donor's attention and moving the relation-ship forward.

The typical Donor Experience Officer meets with more than 200 prospects each year, but also secures gifts from 700 people, demonstrating that it is possible to convert gifts and grow donors even without a face-to-face meeting, virtual or otherwise.

Virtual Visits

Grinna's perspective on digital experience officers relies on initial visits via digital channels, of course, and many prospective donors prefer this. When thinking about your focus as a fundraiser, you know it is useful to consider the background of your prospective donor. As a person who has amassed enough wealth to make sizable charitable gifts, she is likely very, very good at making choices. As we saw with the directions for leveraging mindfulness and other tactics to get the initial visit, be considerate of your prospective donors' efforts to gain focus and optimize their time. As a result, many of us have increasingly found that certain prospective donors are fine with virtual visits. In this context, virtual visits are calls, texts, emails, and video conference calls that move the relationship closer to a decision about a gift. These move prospective donors closer to a yes or no about their potential investment in your organization. While face-to-face visits remain the standard for fundraising, it is useful to assess this standard. Our fundraising, like our banking, is increasingly digital. Cedars-Sinai's Art Ochoa shared that he frequently defaults to texting with prospects with whom he is close. It is efficient and preferred by many.

One of the ironies of the growing reliance on virtual visits is that the same digital technology that supports the visit also distracts participants at every turn. Once you are no longer at that lunch or across the couch from your prospect, how much of their attention do you think you're receiving? Most of the busiest people in the world have become masters at multi-tasking while on Zoom, so why will your virtual visit be different? This should not suggest that virtual visits will not work; EverTrue and others have shown they can for their clients. Instead, you need to be realistic and heighten your focus.

The advice for improving focus leans into brain science, mindfulness, and essential communications strategy. Whether by phone or video call, and particularly via email, you lose the potential to glean body language and subtle nuances in the communications. But there are other options to leverage.

- **Set up for success.** What you do before virtual visits will set the stage. The writing of Gladwell, the Heath brothers, and Kahneman on decisions and bias show there is reason to believe that brand, personal connections, and other nearly primordial aspects of the relationship with the prospect are at play. Much of this has nothing to do with you, but you need to take it into account. Can you prompt certain thoughts and preempt others with work you do before the call? Perhaps sending videos that help them reminisce or other materials that draw them in? Agendas can be tricky and feel too formal, but showing your prospect the plan for the conversation can set minds at ease.

- **Confirm expectations.** One component of focusing on prospects in advance of meetings is that it will keep you from being (as) surprised by the prospect's decisions. A starting point for channeling that behavior is to give the prospect clear details about your virtual visit. This might mean a clear and compelling reason to continue reading an email or a pre-meeting agenda and participant list for the prospect. For virtual visits to work, you need them to have an idea of what you are hoping will come from the visit, and, ideally, that outcome should be to the prospect's benefit.

- **Short and sweet.** Our attention spans are purportedly shrinking. It is possible that a carefully orchestrated and lengthy video call (or a very long email, for that matter) is necessary to engage the prospect. Most of what we know about how people think and make choices, though, suggests that drawn-out discussions are not effective. Instead, shorter and more targeted discussions will work better.

- **Keep it simple (but not simplistic).** "Short" messages are not always simple. In fact, decoding coy writing or indirect discussions can be maddening, especially if the two parties in the communication are not particularly close. Teams that have established what is called "transactive memory" can finish each other's sentences, but unclear virtual calls can leave the prospect scratching their head. The simplicity you should seek here is of the elegant kind. That is, you should have distilled your messaging to an easy-to-grasp case for support. Ideally, you ask more questions than you make direct statements, allowing the prospect to respond rather than making assumptions about their responses.

This is the ideal time to apply a little causativity to your approach. Causativity, described later in the book, is the intersection of productivity *and* purpose; it's the art of working mindfully. Remember: the leap from productive to causative involves one's dedication to a cause, so to speak. That is, when we move from looking at output from our work to outcomes of our work, we consider the larger impact and the bigger picture. With the bigger picture in mind, we are increasingly causative. So, throughout your digital visit, remind yourself to seek your prospect's causativity, too. This sort of engagement will help you keep them interested and help you home in on what makes them most likely to give.

There are mountains of books on the topic of "getting the visit." A lot of them focus on the notion of the value proposition. It is worth noting that getting the initial visit, setting up digital visits, and generally persuading prospects to participate at all hinges on persuading them of the utility of the contact. For that, be ever-mindful of who that person is, what makes them tick, and why they would accept the discussion in the first place, by including their POV.

Digital visits are here to stay and nuanced but share a lot with the in-person visit. Visits often result from a wide variety of engagement strategies. Next we turn to a discussion of engagement strategies to see what focus looks like when applied to high volume activities like events and broad appeals.

15

Engagement Strategies

MANY FUNDRAISING STRATEGIES are not as direct as cultivation, solicitation, and stewardship of individual donors. Events, volunteer activities, mass communications, and other steps are essential. These activities have the power to create massive amounts of distraction, or underlie and boost the entire fundraising process. When they're viewed systemically and holistically, they fuel incredible results.

Chris's Advancement Ecosystem diagram (Figure 15.1) illustrates the layers of typical nonprofit organizations.

As you get further from the center—the major giving core of most successful nonprofits, to the repeatable annual donor, to the casual constituent—the work becomes higher volume and lower value (at least per contributor). As the volume and counts grow, the need to focus and organize details becomes more important. Indeed, at the outer ring of constituent management activity, the risk of distraction grows substantially. Teams need systems to handle volume and discern value. Every message in the general inbox is a potential donor or distraction. We might be encouraged to take the approach Steve took; remember, he answered every phone call that rang to his office and, fortuitously at least one of those was a whale of a call. That arrangement worked in part because the resources and structure of Steve's team

135

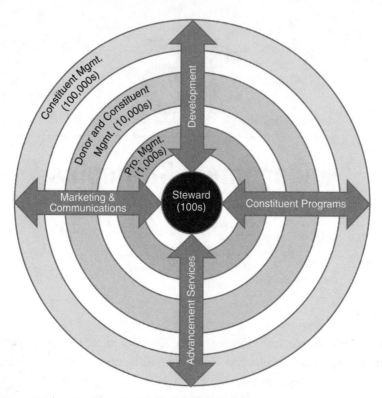

Figure 15.1　Advancement Ecosystem Framework

Source: Chris Cannon, copyright © 2005.

allowed him the time to take that call. Having an overarching, ecosystem-level plan for engagement can help your organization stay focused.

Brand Matters

You can leverage this model to heighten focus on engagement strategies. Having everyone on the same page is a key starting point. To get everyone aligned, start with your brand.

The surest way to engage your base and tailor your messaging to constituents is through your brand. It is also a unifying principle that can help establish focus. If your organization's brand is "the best community hospital in the region," your event fundraising and other activities need to convey this. So should your major and corporate and foundation proposals. Also, simply knowing the look, feel, and language to use in these endeavors (often a marketing and communications assignment and not fundraising per se) can greatly streamline your efforts and get everyone on the same page. That sure sounds like a focused fundraising shop!

Once the brand is clear, work on audiences and messages. Focused fundraising shops' most important audience is their board and closest donors, which live at the center of the advancement ecosystem. How is your nonprofit organized? Do you have policies and procedures to help it evolve and drive progress? Do you have the right key stakeholders? This topic—stakeholder engagement—is vitally important to attaining focus. There are also dozens of great books on this topic. These books generally show that without the right key leadership and stakeholders, your team will struggle to get focused as less capable stakeholders lob less meaningful strategies and directives your way. In fact, failed or meaningless directives are common distractions in the "management" category described in the 4 Ms.

Get Your Engagement Game Plan

With messaging in place, structure engagement for success. If your organization has a viral campaign, have a plan to deal with viral volume. Too many gift batches to handle is your prize. Remember, overload is the point, not the problem.

A good engagement team varies by nonprofit type. Stewardship and donor relations are always needed, as is some level of event management. Marketing and communications may live in the fundraising orbit or at the organization level. Annual giving is a lifeblood for current-use cash and your future pipeline. Social media management is increasingly necessary. Membership, alumni relations, grateful patients, and some other groups less focused on major giving and more focused on retaining the interest of prospective future donors are in this group, too. As with any "practices that are best" model, your team's structure and planning should accommodate all the nuances of your circumstances.

With your brand and team structure in mind, turn to tactics. Written and digital communications are too often late or too shallow because the time to focus on them is snapped up by other urgent items. Stop allowing that, in part by making sure all of those work products align with the biggest possible mission and message you can deliver. How might content you are writing, posting on social media, emailing to people, and committing to the airwaves motivate brand-new donors to give bigger-than-ever gifts? How does all this work hang together? If you are not asking that question, no one else will. If you are not careful, the means ("great-looking appeal, Ed!") will become the end ("last year, we were proud to deliver great-looking new appeals!") rather than advancing your mission, bringing in new donors, and seeing on-hand cash increase.

At the individual and organization levels, all the segments of a robust fundraising effort—prospecting, data and gift management, analytics, and end-to-end engagement—benefit from mindfulness and attention to systemic solutions. Engagement efforts, from the very high volume and digital to the personalized and manual, matter and will add up to greater outcomes for your organization. Where you and your team can RAISE your sights, you will see better results. You will experience causativity—where your purpose and productivity align. To sustain this level of focus, we turn next to operations.

16

Fundraising Operations

ALTHOUGH YOU MAY not oversee operations or work directly in the operations area, it's important to understand it. Mutual understanding between operations team members and fundraisers leads to higher levels of focus. Without understanding, operations is too often where inspiration perishes.

Efficient operations rely on a focus-first mentality. The central operational components for fundraising teams—technology, data, business processes, and governance—offer clear paths to enhance focus and achieve better results for the whole organization.

Technology Change and Operations

Technology change has been vitally important to fundraising operations. The advent of databases for relationship management in the 1970s and 1980s, followed by better systems with better reporting to support decision-making in the 1990s and 2000s, followed by the current state of CRM, social engagement, and machine learning realities have all been positive trends for professional fundraising.

Chris's 2011 book went into detail on the idea of the "iPhone problem," which remains germane in understanding the pressures on operations teams to keep up with consumer-experience-driven expectations. We use smartphones (a misnomer, really, "phones" now are more like digital extensions of our shared and personal experiences and preferences) and wearables to store many things we would have forgotten or kept on paper, in our heads, or among our people through aural history, sometimes in the form of what Daniel Wegner called "transactive memory." We all want that information in databases, but how is it going to get there, who is going to integrate it all, and who is going to make sense of it?

Here's how many operations teams view data management:

- **Data entry is not going away.** The artificial/augmented/actionable intelligence segment these days is a terrific example of the complexity we face. Simply typing an email in Outlook (or a text, for that matter) will offer up sometimes spot-on sentence completion features. It is neat, but it is devoid of context. The services and features are better, yet there is still much missing. It's not safe to assume data entry is going away any time soon, although you may elect to outsource that work sooner than you think.
- **People need to review data.** As an example, about 5,000 words in this book were created via speech-to-text service on an iPhone. Waiting for kids at dance and soccer can do funny things to a fundraising professional. You would never know which paragraphs these were. Why? Because they largely needed to be rewritten. The tech is cool and it is close, but it needs human touch.
- **Timing matters.** A sobering example is the case of an organization in the Midwest that was an early adopter of QR codes … like 10-years-ago early. This enterprising team slapped QR codes on billboards, at bus stops, on buck slips in mailings, and lots of other places. It was a dud: zero opens. No one used the QR code for that whole campaign. Flash forward to 2021 and, due to digital menu provisioning at nearly every restaurant in the world, QR codes are ubiquitous. Their use is cemented in our consumer experiences; these days, that same Midwestern nonprofit organization would be wise to revisit the use of those codes.
- **Be wary of the chicken-egg market challenge**. Is there more content because there is more tech to house it? Or, did storage

capacity expand, allowing for more content? We all seem to want 4K soccer/football/baseball/ballet on our screens, which changed the expectations of our webpages that are competing for eyeballs with companies that have $1 trillion-plus market valuations. Tech is changing us and we generally seem to want the change, but not at the cost of poorer attention spans and instant overload.

Contemporary, cloud-based, highly integrated CRMs are a far cry from their database ancestors. However, real people are still needed to manage and maintain them. And ultimately, these tools are still just a means to an end.

Give Gift Administration Its Due

Just as fundraising operations depend on technology, they also depend on gift administration as the bedrock of our fundraising shops. Bemoaned for periodic errors, gift administration, sometimes called gift processing, is often not well understood. Managers want to speed it up *and* avoid mistakes, lamenting a lack of attention to detail. "How could they miss their new address?" "We can't afford to screw up the donor's acknowledgment!"

Often, gift processing falls prey to the forced-focus misperception. Mistakes are not a failure of willpower or effort. Error is more likely to come from task switching. Task switching is a general challenge of how your brain processes the switch from one topic to another. If you examine your current gift processes, you will likely find a host of switches built into the steps team members are expected to replicate. Move between gift and constituent records. Scan details for the financial deposit. Start producing receipts in this tool over here. We generally are telling gift processing team members to think about too many things and not enough, all at the same time.

To add focus, organize gift processing into four parts: intake, batching, entry, and finalization. This framework illustrates the flow of gifts, pledges, and other such transactions in any fundraising shop. Starting with this framework to gain focus adds clarity to the way team members can work. Two reasons that this approach helps are that it is mutually exclusive and exhaustive. Any good typology should be.

There is a clear start, a clear finish, and while there are handoffs between the steps, most shop's processes will complete each step before moving onto the next.

Starting with **intake**, focus can be improved in a few key ways. First, focus requires identifying priorities. As gifts are gathered during the intake activity of a nonprofit organization, lay out a prescribed prioritization of which contributions matter most, while acknowledging that every contribution matters to your organization. Essentially your team needs to start with a matrix of who the donors are, the purpose of the gift, the amount of the contribution, and other such details specific to your nonprofit. Second, during intake, highly focused organizations will have a prioritized set of contributions that they always handle first, pay the closest attention to, and connect to the bigger picture of the organization. This last step is critically important because in balancing accuracy, speed, and volume, gift administration teams are often overwhelmed. They need focused direction. Third, documented intake steps allow multiple team members to play a role or job share. This has the joint benefit of allowing teams to spread the load and give everyone some headspace to think about what they are handling, while also ensuring that priorities are applied.

At the **batch** stage, there are some additional tactics that will help increase focus. One of those tactics requires providing easy-to-use, easy-to-see, automated-not-manual coding steps in processes. If you pick up a pen to write on every check, your chances for focus are low. Instead, use writable PDFs, multiple computer screens for digital document viewing, and online forms for batch and deposit form creation. The organization of gifts into segments needs to be determined by the rules set in advance and those rules should drive the focus of the team.

The **entry** stage in highly focused shops is where streamlining matters. For most shops, half or more of all gifts and pledges can be auto-loaded, reviewed using exception management reports, and other simplifications. This is where the notion of "entry" starts to lose some meaning, as many gifts are not "entered" by team members. On the other hand, at entry for "front of the line" contributions, team members' focus is heightened by color-coded flags and triggers, ideally of the digital variety but perhaps just a brightly colored cover letter with context and details. Such gifts are not to be allowed to sit on desks or in inboxes. Here, entry must be done accurately (and first, before gifts of lesser importance), so often-inefficient multiple checkpoints and reviews are worth the effort for the smaller batch of transactions.

The last stage of the process, **finalization**, has two main components: receipts and reconciliation. The stewardship-side work will also have acknowledgment components, filing, and perhaps some new coding of the database, such as new membership calculations. The finance-side work will require careful setup of both data components and automation of a feed of gift and pledge data to the organization's general ledger. Focused fundraising teams have automated almost all of this. Additionally, they use exception reporting to find issues, and use acknowledgments to handle the high-value "exceptions."

You Cannot Improve a Process You Do Not Value

Focused direction depends on valuing the work. Far too often, the challenge around gift processing is not exactly the lack of focus, but rather devaluation of the tasks. Gift administration is placed low on the priority list and low in the organization's structure. The very people who handle our biggest gifts are typically paid the least and overloaded the most during the busiest times of the year. This is a problem.

So, beyond adding focus to intake, batch, entry, and finalization steps, focused teams value the work by adding analysis. Analysis here goes well beyond the double- and triple-checking we often see in processing shops that serve to create more work. In fact, Chris argues regularly that to triple-check something is to poorly design the double check. That is, triple-checking means the process is not working. More checking seems needed because of eyebrow-raising edge cases, but rarely does the third check add value. If the triple check is where problems are caught, do not celebrate. Fix the double check.

The opportunity is to steer toward analysis, especially of key high-value and high-volume activities. For high-value donations, this means understanding the donation, the context, the related parties from the donor's side, and the interested stakeholders at your organization. Focused fundraising teams have established priorities to identify high-value items. Generally, do not automate entry steps for high-value donations; handle them with great care. Compare each piece of information in the transaction with the database of record. Encourage team members to raise a hand or send an email where neat, new, or potentially useful details are learned.

For high-volume activities, insert a lighter level of analysis at the summative and exception-seeking reporting that the system can generate for review. A highly focused team can trust that their processes will allow a global import of thousands of, say, phone-a-thon pledges, without review in advance. Instead, dashboards of quality assurance queries and results can be reviewed as an exception log *if* there are any. The analyst role is assigned to patterns and processes that find meaningful problems and then use the system itself to validate effectiveness. Add in a routine, periodic audit of the processes and the team can overcome overload and remain focused.

Gift administration can contribute to focus. But before it does, it needs to be valued. Keep this in mind as we turn to related operational topics. What you will find is that the themes in this section— prioritization, structure, emphasis on analysis, and workflow (like the intake > batch > entry > finalization framework)—repeat. Let's turn next to governance.

Focus from (and on) Governance

Many of us have experienced frenetic bosses or boards whose directives lead to a great amount of work with sometimes paltry results. (Remember, management is one of the 4 Ms.) Here we will learn how to leverage governance, that is, the rules of the road, to help your organization become less distracted and more focused. It's tempting to think that governance is only the concern of top leaders, but in focused fundraising organizations it's everyone's business.

Good data and technology governance is a snoozefest for some. For others, it's one "light bulb" moment after the next. Regardless of your interest in it, it is important. Why does good governance support focused fundraising? Governance allows an organization to concentrate its efforts on the proper potential returns on the investment of time, resources, and energy. It allows an organization to establish and follow an effective and efficient division of labor that harnesses each team member's best contributions. Governance ensures that the entire team knows the rules of the game. This means that team members know what should and should not be in their purview, because the governance plan articulates ownership and activity expected across the fundraising organization. Governance also provides authority to those in the organization responsible for activities, such as a data list used for mailing or a prospect assignment. Unclear ownership is a frequent frustration.

For instance, far too many fundraising shops have said that nearly every mailing list produced for events or solicitations requires some manual review, often by a gift officer who is concerned about data integrity or accuracy. Tedious reviews distract frontline fundraisers from their top priorities. Yet, painstaking manual reviews are so common that many teams add double checks, forgetting that even a single check could be a misuse of time. In a good governance environment, an organization has a chance to break inefficient cycles. In this case, better governance establishes expectations for who owns the caliber and quality of the data points and data output. In addition, those responsible for better data quality and output would be empowered to ensure common problems are rectified wherever possible.

Governance is an "all in" affair. Leadership needs to buy in. Finance and IT teams, as well as compliance offices, need to agree. Operations teams who tend to own the data and systems need to accept their role to administer many aspects of governance. Frontline fundraisers need to understand the rationale and applications, as well as how to operate within the structures. There are a lot of moving parts. Many of you have shops represented by perhaps dozens of different departments that have varied opinions that need to be considered during the process of establishing governance. Resource scarcity can be a challenge, as some groups may view such rules as threatening to their strategies. Staffing and leadership changes endemic to fundraising can make such programs hard to maintain. In short, governance can be quite difficult to enact. The Focused Fundraising Maturity Model in Chapter 19 can help, but the work is significant and complex.

When faced with a complicated challenge like building a governance program at your organization, starting simply is often the best path. Simple here does not mean simplistic. Rather, simple means elegant, something that can be viewed as necessary while being clear to all parties involved. Often, governance initiatives become overly complicated and those complications lead to failure.

So, how should your organization go about establishing governance? In line with an elegant approach, you need the following factors represented in your plan.

- First, you need a stakeholder analysis of the organization. This can become quite complicated; however, it can also be done in a matter of an hour. In this analysis your team needs defined roles.
- Second, your plan needs to establish the scope of governance. Good governance needs to cover topics like overall constituent engagement, technology application management, gift administration, prospect development assignment and solicitation, direct response and list and data use, and key data point management, such as name and address updates. For all of these areas, explain who does what and why. Saying what is often unspoken brings the clarity necessary to remain focused.
- Third, with the stakeholders and a scope identified, establish a team to work through the details of the plan. Empower the team to come to agreement on the questions of data and process and ownership that lead to the clarity of activity and process necessary to avoid the risk of a free-for-all fundraising environment.

Some of you reading this have already participated in and established governance models. Your approach was perhaps as straightforward as indicated here, yet often there are significant obstacles. For those of you with governance in place, you know that it is a dynamic process. For those of you who have not yet established a governance approach for your team, realize that even if it is a challenge culturally or organizationally, the benefits far outweigh the costs. And, as indicated, you will need to be prepared to refine, adjust, and improve your governance. It is worth the effort. Figure 16.1 shows the parts of a great governance ecosystem.

Breaking down the components of data and technology governance is an effective way to establish rules of the game. There are countless, interesting books on the notion of governance. Hirschman's classic,

Figure 16.1   Governance Model Components

Exit, Voice, and Loyalty, about the decline in firms, organizations, and states, lays out how to strengthen any group along the way. In summary, governance stems from you building a path toward "loyalty" (i.e., following the rules) by allowing some to "voice" their concerns or even "exit" along the way. Bend in some areas while not breaking in others; otherwise, the incentive to exit become too attractive. Viewing governance as a one-time, document-creating exercise will get it wrong. Instead, view it like a working, living, breathing road map. To use the Jim Collins *Good to Great* metaphor, monitor who is on (and getting off) the bus while en route to your destination.

At the organization level, your team can view these components strategically and concisely to deliver a workable solution for the whole group.

- **Organization (aka the Team).** From the perspective of the whole, perception and change readiness are essential. Who should be involved? What stakeholders are important and why? What timing, urgency, and relevancy does this work have for the whole? A team of one can start governance efforts. Organizational buy-in is key to finishing them. In order to drive focus from the team, you need to make sure the governance effort is viewed as legitimate and authentic at every step.
- **Policies.** Writing down your organization's practices is essential. If you cannot write them, it begs the question of whether they exist or are some wholly aural semi-management guidance. Gaps in what is written can be a deliverable of the data and technology governance committee, but too many gaps by the end of the effort will not give the guidance needed to direct people toward the preferred behaviors.
- **Catalogs.** In addition to knowing what policies are available, knowing what options of data exist is critical to establishing great governance. This ties to sources some, but the idea at this point is that a healthy record of "what is out there" gives the committee a place to start, looking for gaps and validating what is working. This is true for data, technology application, and other resources (like training aids).
- **Definitions.** Shared language may be the most subtle yet important aspect of governance. George Lakoff's work on typologies and language available (or not) to explain things is essential to adding focus. If you want your board to trust the quarterly reports, you must use the same labels time after time. This is beyond a technical data dictionary. This is a glossary of terms and a brand and style guide. With everyone "singing from the same hymn book," focus will naturally increase as confusion and questions decrease.
- **Sources.** The complexity of governance is partly defined by the number of inputs. For political systems, representative voting may present more complexity than direct constituent voting, but it may be needed. The same goes for governance of data and technology on campuses and across organizations. So, while you catalog what is "out there," you also need to add context to the nature of the source. Issues like legal status of source owners, data

directionality, the "single source of truth," and others make knowing and understanding sources a crucial part of great governance.

- **Quality.** Great governance points your team to the things to measure and the definitions of quality that are important to your organization. Quality is a tricky thing. One person's anecdotal mistake is another person's fireable offense (and we wish we were kidding!). Defining this for your organization, how the team will achieve high levels of it, and how to define "high levels" are all part of the work to complete. This also is part of assessing your standards.
- **Operations and Processes.** These details—how to create a new database record, who owns what parts and how a non-owner shares information, what data files are fed where and how automated that work is—reflect the day-to-day reality of good governance. If the policies are written but no one follows them, your governance will suffer. Processes need to be operationalized and institutionalized to ensure their long-term use and effectiveness.
- **Security and Permissions.** While processes are the functional outcome of great governance, access to (parts of) those processes, the data in use, or the applications in place are equally important. In many ways, once a governance committee has handled the previous items, this one and ongoing process improvements become the chief assignment to the committee. Issues around authorizing access and vetting new technology applications or data usage become the monthly agenda items to ensure good governance.

Two final notes about how great governance helps organizations focus. First, governance evolves; it will take time and iteration to get right and then ongoing refinement over time. Second, governance is also a management issue. All the automation in the world will not talk to Ed about constantly trying to buy new software that the committee has not vetted or approved. The policies, rooted in strategic thinking and resource management fundamentals, should guide the conversation, though. If you have good-to-maybe-great governance, no one should be surprised to be reminded of the rules of the game.

Areas with significant flux in handling outliers—data management and reporting—are the next topic to consider in building focus for your organization. The mundane aspects of day-to-day data management will become more clearly central to establishing a focused fundraising shop. For starters, governance helps determine who is allowed to solicit your donors, when, and how, which then makes strategic information more focused.

17

Strategic Information Management

THE MANAGEMENT OF data and the consumption of that data are intertwined. They are two sides of the same coin. Both data entry and business intelligence, for that matter, are complementary and ongoing. With clients, Chris likens strategic information management work to "shoveling sand on the beach." It is never-ending work (but at least the view is good!). There is purpose and value in the work. The more mindful one is about using data, the better.

Priming Principled Professionals

When Chris worked at the Saint Louis Zoo, an amazing cultural shift was occurring in America. Legalized gambling was moving from Vegas, Reno, and Atlantic City to all (the riverways) of America. New, profitable, and earnestly community-minded casinos opened in the St. Louis area and made the obvious overtures to the Zoo, given the 6 million eyeballs that roamed its grounds each year. This was a tricky situation for the Zoo's leadership, some of whom opposed organized gambling. Yet, one of the Zoo's best donors had been Anheuser-Busch, the world's leading beer brewer. How could the Zoo say no to funding from casinos and say yes to the adult beverage industry? On the other hand, also-legal tobacco companies had been excluded from supporting the Zoo and other cultural institutions in the region. In these scenarios, principles matter. For the record, at the time, the Zoo said, "No thanks."

By the Zoo taking a stand, the fundraising team knew what was important. The decision helped the development team close off an area of potential distraction. Strategic information management begins with principles like this. And principles require shared definitions. Governance, as we discussed earlier, defines how complex gifts are handled and who has access to what data and tools. Transparency is important. Strategic information management means documenting and codifying these practices. Your data reinforce your principles.

Righteousness of Recording Data

We have all heard the saying that "if it's not in the database, it didn't happen." This is a favorite among prospect development teams. Chris can hear himself from the late 1990s imploring his colleagues: "Hey, guys. Please get your contact reports into the database!" This was sometimes followed by "Please," then "Pretty please," then "C'mon ... this is my job," à la Professor Jennings in the movie *Animal House*. In all seriousness, this point is critical: *persuading others to contribute is essential for focused fundraising*. However, it is also one of the points most ignored by fundraisers, particularly those who feel that they are beyond busy: **getting data into a centralized system is also essential for focused fundraising.**

But who has the time, right? What if others are not doing it, anyhow? And what if the development leader's proposals, contact reports, and data updates never make it into the database? A common complaint among fundraisers is that not only does the head of [insert rogue unit name] not record details, but funding still comes in, so who cares? This is not just frontline officers with their prospect portfolios. Many, like Chris, have their "piles of shame," which are essentially all of the data updates being saved for a day that will never arrive.

The cost of this distracted, overwhelmed reality is substantial. Incomplete records, inaccurate donor profiles, missed opportunities.

Missing and "mishandled" data can lead to lots and lots of shame, defensiveness, and distraction. However, it really is righteous for every fundraiser to make the time to record what they are doing and learning. Three immutable reasons for recording details help every fundraiser prioritize this work.

- **First, the cost of bad or missing data is significant.** There are real costs in staff time and tactical opportunity costs when an organization cannot call or email its constituency. Sometimes these data are truly unknown, but too often, unfocused, overly busy team members simply have not yet shared those data points. It is also important to consider that the data being learned does not belong to the fundraiser. Those data belong to the organization for whom the fundraiser is working. This means that every email and cell phone number in an iPhone but not the database is a problem. It is the employee's responsibility to solve that problem (ideally with easy-to-use tech).
- **Second, the impact of not knowing what has happened with donors and prospects diminishes strategies and puts relationships at risk.** We all have those stories. You know, the one where a gift officer asks a prospect for a four-figure gift at lunch only to learn that the vice president planned to visit that prospect about a naming gift in a week. The lack of sharing data to coordinate these engagements is a real risk. Or, perhaps one team member knows that a couple's divorce is imminent while another asks the couple to join a volunteer campaign board. You get the picture … incomplete data can and do lead to problems.
- **Third, the long-term benefits have untold potential.** We shared earlier in the book that at Yale, Michael proposed their vision for strategic information management through the lens of the future of the University. The "we can raise more with more data" message helped but was not as convincing. The "we need the whole picture" message made sense, but the gift officer core was dedicated to learning these details whether they were in their systems or not. What really resonated for Michael's team was the future-focused message but not the near future, not even for the span of a comprehensive campaign. What resonated was the idea that

these data points weave a fabric of engagement that will tell a story in 200 or 300 years. Records management became a solemn duty for the whole team so that Yale as a foundational institution for American society and the global Academy—the researchers and academics making the world a better place—would be positioned and remembered appropriately. That is a powerful way to make recording data a righteous act, rather than simply a mundane task.

It takes commitment to build confidence in data. A gift officer who has dialed three wrong numbers in a row may lose faith in the data and database and stop relying on centralized records. This is where the mentality of "Okay. We will fix it" can help where the culture fits. Incomplete stories about donors and their relationships may lead the team to use central resources even less, or at least to rework the prospect research and other efforts due to a lack of trust. The posterity angle for data management is bound to stir some collective action problems, whereby staff cannot be made to care because the impact of that sort of work is such a far-off consideration. Although records management will forever remain a bore to most, focused fundraisers keep the faith. Relationships depend on good data.

In focused fundraising, there are surprisingly similar mechanics in top shops. Data points are gathered along the way, stored centrally, and instructional to building relationships. Good data, good notes from the last visit, and good teamwork to gather facts and insights all lead to better discussions and results. And, as boring as it may be, it starts with shared commitment to data. Imagine if the doctor were to arrive at your exam room, ask you to reweigh, retake your blood pressure and temperature, and then ask you to recount what you remember from your last visit. Bad data can lead to these sorts of inefficient experiences, which is why organizational policies and practices must reinforce data management.

At Yale, the advancement operations team looks long-term. The team realized that the future of philanthropy at Yale required more attention to the whole constituency and, specifically, better and better data to connect with constituents and to conduct analytics. The idea was that great operations now would secure the future of Yale not just for this campaign and the next, but for the next *century and the next*.

That is, the team used the argument that better data now will mean institutional legacy for 2330, too.

The following tips and tricks cut through the tedium of data management:

- **Prioritize points.** Some data, like a good cell phone number or a prospect's employment details, matter way more than others. Get these high-value details into the system as soon as possible.
- **Build a collection process.** Even small shops can make data capture easier. Some systems are actually pretty good, and so training and database rights should be explored. Others are not helpful, but even an Excel file, a PDF form, or a shared email address can be an improvement to the often-scattershot approaches. Using integration tools with, say, email applications can make a huge difference.
- **Small bursts.** Unless you do this work for a living, try to limit data work to 15 minutes. This sort of concentrated effort will result in better work and less consternation.
- **Your front-of-the-line.** Just as distractions derail, data volume can overload us, leading to unfocused, ad hoc working patterns. Apply the Pareto principle, aka the 80/20 rule, where 80% of your results come from 20% of your efforts, described later in the book. The Pareto principle leads you to bring the important records and data points to the front of the line.
- **Calendar your work.** Establish a "time box" for data entry. Calendaring your data management is the very definition of time boxing and, more important, discipline in this area can keep your team on track to do what needs to be done and not worry about what needs to be done later.
- **Diminish distractions.** When updating details and dealing with data management, turn your phone to "do not disturb." Turn off alerts from your computer. Keep background noise like a TV to a minimum or turn it off altogether. You will go faster and be more precise as a result of staying focused.

In many ways, great individual behavior starts with great organizational governance and practices. Great data management is the aggregate of focused work per person on the team. While it is vital to focus on data going into your systems, information delivery and consumption are just as important to focused fundraising.

From Data In to Data Out

In just a few short years, a reporting revolution has happened under our noses. A "report" used to be a formatted aggregation of data points and calculations to inform the reader of some historic, descriptive outcomes. These were generally not automated, not integrated across data sets, not live and interactive, and not very visually engaging. A "report" might mean a "list," or a "summary," or a "comparison." Reports were static and not terribly useful.

In the past decade, the notion of "business intelligence," or BI, started to shape our view of how we understand and use information. "Reporting" became a subset of the deliverables in a really robust BI environment, yet the idea of a "report" persisted, even though it might now mean a simple list of data, a calculated comparison of data points, an automated onscreen image of data that allowed the user to slice and dice details and make better decisions. In fact, the notion of "decision support" (first stated by MIT's Sloan School of Management researchers in the 1970s) took hold in the corporate world well before its use in the nonprofit sector. By now, the idea that data could help make better decisions has taken hold for nonprofit organizations.

More recently, the prevalence and power behind data visualization tools, data warehouses, and other technical frameworks for reporting have created a further refinement: we have moved from building reports to consuming information. That is, in the recent past, reporting meant that one generated either a list into Excel or a static $8\frac{1}{2}{\times}11$-inch report output to learn answers to questions. Now, though, static reports are being replaced by real-time, onscreen, drillable dashboards and visualizations, where the source data details can be viewed as needed. In top shops, professionals are using the directions obtained from their dashboards (or metrics or dynamic onscreen lists) to make decisions and support their work. It is a subtle difference in some ways, but it is a powerful one. What was once a printed report (or emailed attachment) is now available onscreen, dynamic, and up-to-date, ready to be consumed and acted upon by savvy decision-makers.

So, why does this matter to a focused fundraiser? How you choose to consume information on a daily basis is critically important to homing in on the topics and trends for that moment, while eschewing distractions.

In our research and interviews, we very frequently learned that bad reporting is an enormous distraction. Ideally, your shop provides you with an effective information delivery environment. We refer to this as a "FACT"-based ecosystem. In top-notch arrangements, information delivery is well formatted (F) so that users know where to look and have trust in the quality of the work. The data are accurate (A), which means they are viewed as correct, but this also implies that all involved shared definitions and an understanding of the components of each report. Complete (C) data sound obvious, yet many fundraising professionals have to work at getting their information together in one place with all of the data points aggregated. The last piece, and one in which sophisticated information delivery environment excel, is providing timely (T) data for decision support. Far too many fundraising professionals work in an environment in which the "final" numbers require an extra week's worth of review and massaging. In addition, too many shops require hours or weeks to compile such data.

Those whose reporting environments are not FACT-based are swimming against a stream of distraction. Information consumers will have many questions: "Are these data up-to-date?" "Does this include the Johnsons' planned gift?" "Why do I not see the XYZ Corporation listed?" Each of these questions is a nail in the coffin of focused fundraising.

The good news is that better and better information is within your reach. Remember Chapter 9's analytics discussion with Nathan Chappell? It gave us hope in more viable AI and machine learning models. Here are the questions to answer to realize the promise of greatly improved reporting and decision support:

- How much trust do we have in our data?
- How do we share definitions about our data?
- Can we access all of our data?

- How effective are our tools at revealing trends and insights in data?
- How many team members use these tools to guide daily or weekly decisions?
- What improvements should we continue to explore?

With the paradigm shift from reporting to information delivery and consumption, you are better positioned to discern what you need and what you do not. Focus depends on being a discerning consumer. We now turn to maturity models, practical and powerful tools to use in raising your team's sights.

18

The Power of Maturity Models

MEANINGFUL CULTURE CHANGE happens when everyone gets real. Evolution does not proceed from wishful thinking. So, in terms of focus in your organization, is it safe to ask: How focused are we today?

Highly focused organizations consistently ask the questions: Where are we now in our development of focused fundraising? How well do we serve our mission? Where might we improve? A team that is "all over the place" is not focused. Teams that are pulled "in a million directions" are not focused. Being honest does not mean being overly critical, however. What helps is to have a reference point because it is almost certain that there is an organization less focused than yours! This is where maturity models can help.

Maturity Models

The challenges that affect us all individually—the 4 Ms, the tech tug, instant overload—impact organizations, too. Nonprofit organizations are besieged by distractions. The impact of the nonprofit starvation cycle, the damage done by low overhead demands, and the nuanced history of nonprofit missions, cases for support, and giving patterns all cloud decisions and create complexity for nonprofits, feeding into the constant craziness of nonprofit life.

Maturity models organize the complexity and normalize it. Because culture change and organizational improvements take time, they are often subject to the "Boss effect." The Boss effect is that the organization will only be as focused as the Boss. If the Boss is all over the place, or absent, or too controlling, or whatever, then the organization cannot evolve. While this may be the case, bringing a maturity model into the conversation can be a welcome dose of reality for all concerned—even the Boss. Maturity models are not about getting quickly from point A to point B. They are about realizing where you as an organization are in a process and maturing together. These models can be a way to neutralize criticism and focus on the characteristics that are typical, but that get in the way of higher levels of focus. It can be helpful to be reminded that your organization is a lot like a number of others, even if you all want to improve further.

The Focused Fundraising Maturity Model (FFMM) explained in the next chapter was inspired by a long lineage of maturity and capability models. Capability Maturity Models first emerged in the 1980s. In *Encyclopedia of Information Systems*, David Olson writes that the first references to maturity models were created by the Software Engineering Institute at Carnegie Mellon University. The five-level model started with a Level 1 organization being ad hoc with few systems, that is, "all over the place." Level 2 organizations have processes limited by individual controls. Level 3 organizations institutionalize their work and spread capacity across more team members. Level 4 teams regularly deliver expected outcomes and have time and capacity to refine and analyze their work. Level 5 organizations go even further in optimizing their work.

In the Capability version from the 1980s, government procurement experts created a continuum from which they could gauge bidders' capacity for brand-new computer technology areas. The earliest model highlighted that some bidders' capacity seemed ad hoc and episodic while others seemed repeatable or even optimized. In a world that was being created every day in line with Moore's Law about computing power expansion, this model made sense of very complex organizational evaluations. The trick was recognizing that any organization could sit along the continuum; the position was not pejorative, it was instructive. Organizations could grow into more and more capable teams. Finding Level 5 companies was the initial purpose, but the long-term application created a framework to instruct organizations on how to grow. Fundamentally, Level 5 organizations in that very first Capability Maturity Model are focused; they are achieving their purpose and optimizing their efforts to deliver even more future value to their missions.

Those first maturity models highlighted a way of focusing an organization on where it wants to be ("Level 5") while recognizing where the organization is right now. These models provide a path in the metaphor used in the Heath brothers' book *Switch*. In *Switch*, change is viewed as needing a path for both the elephant (emotional, slow-moving parts of an organization) and the rider (logical, change-driving parts of the team pushing the organization forward). A path sets a general direction, but is not prescriptive. There is substantial literature about how organizations (and individuals) can achieve a balanced, forward-thinking approach to strategy when the path is clear.

A decade ago, Don Hasseltine, now a senior vice president with Aspen Leadership Group, shared with Chris his approach to a maturity model. In his CASE white paper "Performance Management Maturity Model: Raising the Bar of Fundraising Performance," Hasseltine asked: "What do I [the fundraising executive] need to do to create an environment to achieve optimum performance, regardless of the institution's history, investment in fundraising, and mission?" Hasseltine's approach recommended a five-tier model: initiating, refining, managing, strategizing, and optimizing. Hasseltine observed that "every department on your team is best served when it follows the model's levels in sequence. This allows you to see where your current teams' maturity levels conflict, where and in whom you should invest, and how to overcome 'organizational roadblocks.'" The idea of "optimum performance" was another way of thinking about focused fundraising.

Hasseltine's model requires each element of the fundraising organization—leadership, major giving, annual giving and direct response, and planned giving, operations, stewardship, alumni relations, membership, and other units—to expand their performance in sequence. Separate efforts, such as annual giving and events, cannot be too far in front of or behind others. On the operations front, Hasseltine stated: "Data drive our business, and having a first-rate system is critical to success." All of these areas work together, symbiotically.

Major Giving Maturity Model

Chris and his Zuri Group colleague Kate Nimety crafted a similar model, the Major Giving Maturity Model (MGMM). This model, designed for organizations with multiple departments or units with varying levels of resources and capacity, allows each team to recognize where they are on the continuum of increasingly sophisticated fundraising strategies. The Major Giving Maturity Model provides a clear path to move closer and closer to becoming an optimized principal and major giving shop while respecting the utility of less lucrative and less efficient fundraising tactics common to smaller and newer fundraising shops.

Consider the MGMM in Figure 18.1. In it, you see that most nonprofits start as, essentially, volunteer efforts. At this Level 1 stage, cost per dollar raised looks great because there is no payroll! However, the ability to raise substantial money to support your mission during this phase is typically limited. Level 2 typically relies on events that tend to be high effort and low(er) impact than higher levels in the model. However, one never knows when that event attendee will become a significant major giving donor. The next level—direct response, Level 3—moves the organization into direct mail, digital philanthropy, phone-a-thon, and other tactics. Here, the notion of "advanced annual giving" takes shape through donor societies and efforts to engage donors to give more and bigger gifts. This level contains more repeatable efforts and should build a base of donors to grow through good operational practices.

The focus as we move up the model shifts toward answering "should we do this thing?" instead of simply "can this thing we do help us generate more money?" Previous levels in the model remain necessary components as the organization matures. Mature major giving shops still need events and email solicitations. Further levels—Level 4 Major

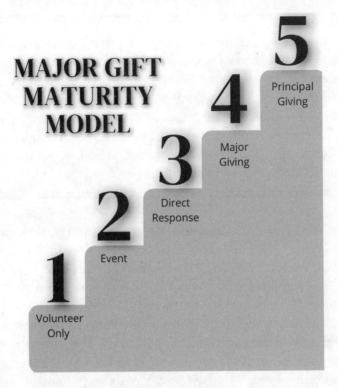

Figure 18.1   Major Giving Maturity Model

Giving and Level 5 Principal Giving—are extensions of similar principles. More and more mature organizations are increasingly effective at doing what should be done, because they are focused at the top of the continuum.

Volunteer fundraising, events fundraising, direct response, major giving, and finally principal giving increasingly focus the organization on results. That is, as the case for support improves and matures (i.e., moving from "as a volunteer, we hope you can give your time" to "as a direct mail donor, please upgrade this year" to "as an invested benefactor in our mission, please consider a $500,000 contribution to …"), elements of the past model stages need to be retained but redirected toward the current of a higher level. Indeed, tactics from less mature stages can be leveraged to great effect, as the Saint Louis Zoo found with carefully crafted events in the 1990s and 2000s preparing new waves of major donors in the 2010s and beyond.

Tracking the genesis of major donors will often lead to event attendance. When Chris worked at the world-famous Saint Louis Zoo, there was a clear pattern that major donors in the 2000s attended specific events in the 1990s. This was expressly because those late 1990s event were expressly cultivation events, even if some money was raised at the event. The events, in effect, were a means to an end. Flash forward two decades and many of the most generous Zoo donors can be shown to have had their start as event attendees.

This model, plus the adoption of a major gift mentality, can align disparate units who, like Hasseltine noted, are not at the same levels. In a recent exercise involving this approach, Chris and his colleague Kate Nimety applied this model to a newly integrated health care system. Ten different hospitals with varying levels of volunteer, event, direct mail, major, and principal giving results and apparatus easily coalesced around the principles in the model. The easy-to-remember "will this help us with major giving?" mantra helped leaders at each hospital jettison some of their "we have always done it this way" activities. This, in turn, added focus and made choices—"Run this event? Create that newsletter? Buy that app?"—easier.

The Focused Fundraising Maturity Model (FFMM) builds on the Major Giving Maturity Model. Whereas many top shops have structured their business units around major and principal giving, just changing the organization chart may not be enough. One way for organizations to move up the model is to focus on the process. They need to recognize the energy to sustain their evolution. Establishing a focused direction is essential.

New and immature organizations tend to not only start their fundraising with volunteer and event efforts, they also sometimes lack the ability to ignore the distractions, which keeps them stuck at the beginning of the model. There are common reasons that, among the 1.56 million nonprofits in America, only a few thousand raise more than $10 million a year. One of the most common limitations is a lack of focus. This is in no way intended to be dismissive of the generous efforts of those running these hundreds of thousands of nonprofits but instead reinforces the idea that an organization must focus on moving up the model and make choices that will result in more significant fundraising outcomes.

The distractions facing most nonprofits are not surprising. A volunteer-led nonprofit is, almost by definition, managed by very well-intentioned people with something else to do. Fundraising is not their job. The mission may be their passion and that will be a source of fundraising success. But, without a mindset that is focused on moving from fun events to dedicated and daily major giving, most nonprofits will remain small and typically volunteer-run. Add to this the all-too-common tendency for new nonprofits to suffer from what is sometimes called "founder's syndrome" (aka, "founderitis") and the potential to stagnate at Level 1 is a real obstacle.

Note that there are of course some incredibly successful high-volume/low-average gift organizations that may not fit the "major giving shop" model. Many of these shops actually also generate substantial major giving results. Organizations can contain all phases of the model. Channeling and prioritizing toward the higher end are the purpose. This is a version of the "yes and ..." improv technique outlined by Camden Morse that we discussed earlier. Does your organization need volunteer fundraising? "Yes, and ... you also need to build a direct mail campaign that feeds a major gift pipeline that results in as many sizable gifts your organization can secure." Does the team need to hold that very time-consuming event in the fall? "Yes, and ... can we make sure that the attendees reflect our deep prospect pool and that we have a clear set of post-event follow-ups to further engage key attendees, including an active effort to get more than just the 'usual suspects' to join us this time?"

19

Focused Fundraising Maturity Model

How DO YOU determine whether focus is improving at your organization? Change can be confused with improvement. Doing a lot can seem like doing something important. So how do you steady your POV? A maturity model for focus, gives you a realistic talking point to RAISE the topic of focus in your organization.

The Focused Fundraising Maturity Model (FFMM) is a standard you can use to support your efforts. Figure 19.1 is a diagram of the FFMM. Your organization will find that, just as you cannot hop from an event-focused Level 2 shop to a principal gift Level 5 shop, the same is true for moving from a wildly distracted organization to an enlightened, focused team. It is those sorts of wild swings that lead to wishful thinking on organizational and personal levels—Chris: "I'm going to be a zero inbox proponent!" Michael: "But, Chris, you have 8,712 unopened emails." "Yes, but it's going to be different this week." Yo-yoing often does more harm than good. A more balanced strategy is to go step-by-step.

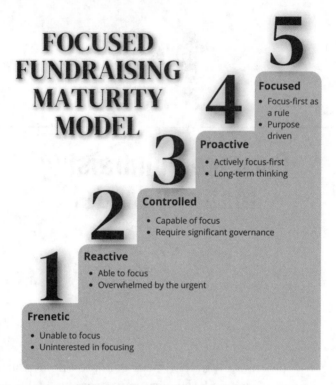

Figure 19.1   Focused Fundraising Maturity Model

These levels likely seem familiar. They are a reflection of our organizational reality and many of our day-to-day personal experiences. We work through the day, sometimes in chaos, often responding to a slew of email, trying to follow protocols to the letter, sneaking in a planful moment or two, and, if we are lucky, achieving nirvana here and there with a genius idea coming to fruition. Our teams are composed of those who are calm in the eye of the storm and those who seem overloaded by the slightest request. As a reminder, organizations (and individuals) can experience all these levels simultaneously across departments (or, as individuals, across areas in our lives). It is important that, in experiencing multiple aspects of the FFMM, all parts of the organization are relatively synchronized around the same levels. Exploring these levels further will make applying the model clearer.

Level 1: Frenetic

We have all been here. Frenetic shops are often a few good decisions and focused activities away from moving to Level 2 and beyond. Part-time staff and volunteer-only, events-driven organizations led by well-intentioned but overwhelmed founders are often found here. They are indicated by poor staffing levels, no staff retention of note, and an inability to secure the work needed to deliver results. Prospecting does not happen yet and there is little long-term thinking. As a result, these organizations suffer the most from the nonprofit starvation cycle.

The path toward maturity starts with getting realistic. Rather than fret about this (or being angry with us for our bluntness), try RAISE. Choose an initial topic from the organization's priorities. What is your POV on the organization's priorities? Spend more time there thoughtfully developing a narrative and approach that will encourage consistency and professionalism. And, while you are at that, you can RAISE another topic: your return on mission. What is your POV on your organization's mission? What do others think? Reporting not just the occasional anecdotes but real trends will help the team move from hectic and distracted to more focused and purposeful. Here are some other topics you can RAISE.

- **RAISE a topic like resources.** If you are about to post your organization's very first part-time director of development, job description, stop! You will not get far with wishful thinking that a fantasy fundraiser is going to magically sprinkle donors like fairy dust.
- **RAISE a topic like fundraising familiarity.** If you fall prey to the three myths and think that fundraising is "begging" (the last thing you want to do on behalf of your nonprofit), take a quick look in the mirror and ask, "If *you* think that, what must a prospective donor think?"
- **RAISE a topic like events.** If you are wondering whether you can pull off the organization's only fundraising event in six months, you are essentially doubting that you have the resources to make an event profitable and worthwhile. Maybe that is a catalyst for alternative ideas.

If you begin to RAISE topics that need focus, you're off to a good start. It will help you advance to Level 2. Remember: be honest about your organization's position. Candor helps.

Level 2: Reactive

At the Reactive level, individuals and teams value the work and want to plan, but the urgent overwhelms the important. Inefficient processes are sketched out to handle volume and issues but are halfway implemented. Documentation is hard to create, due to limited time and to shifting priorities.

Like event fundraising, this is where many stop, because it feels like activity equals progress. "We are all so busy, we must be accomplishing something" is a common leadership-level refrain in these cases. At this stage, how can you better react to and start directing the 4 Ms? How can you RAISE your focus? Here are some pointers for many of us who are much more reactive than we would like:

- **RAISE a topic like your organization's schedule.** What is your POV on the schedule? What do others think? Are schedules respected? How's the accountability with meetings and follow-ups? This can help you identify trends and ebbs and flows of work. Consider asking yourself ahead of major events if you have a contingency plan and can produce what you need in a reasonable time.
- **RAISE a topic like your prospect list.** What's the state of prospects now? Who is thinking about it? Who is thinking about your prospects on a daily or weekly basis? If you have not yet gotten past the reactive stage, it is good to consider your lists and how they're serving your purposes.
- **RAISE a topic like long-term planning.** What's leadership's POV on a plan for this year? For the longer term? It needn't be the dreaded year-long strategic planning process. Inquiring into plans can open up some room for focus. It can be a means to start to gain some traction and control over your environment. These sorts of exercises give you the direction on where and when to say "Yes, and ..." in ways that will help your team mature.

Level 3: Controlled

As you move from mostly reactive to controlled, your team has a chance to look up and out at longer-term priorities. Your team will start to become more focused as a result. There are some key considerations at this stage that are reasonable to tackle. First, governance can be established that takes some of the choices out of the equation. Channels for the organization to react to requests are in place, such as a ticketing system to track work requests and a prioritization effort around budgeting and planning for next year's fundraising efforts. These mirror direct response–oriented fundraising shops. There are checklists. There are request forms. Some of this may seem simple or bureaucratic, but we often find shops that have some of these components but do not follow their own rules.

However, controlled does not necessarily mean creative, and it certainly will not always feel focused. Goals and plans may be in place but more as work plans and budgeting tools than manifestos of purpose. Not surprisingly, such plans skew toward the boring and operational. The inspiration—the wonder and enthusiasm that supports focused fundraising and can captivate attention and focus for hours—is typically in short supply. This makes your work to RAISE your focus tougher, as inspiration cannot be assumed.

Once your team has enough control to start to explore higher levels of focus, there are some key steps to moving beyond merely being responsive (and not just reactive) to stimuli to be able to further optimize the team. Tackling the 4 Ms and other distractions from focus here means that you:

- **RAISE the topic of annual and quarterly planning.** What is driving it? Who is driving it? Might you target new goals? It's especially important to dig into the why for organizational goals. Dig into the Inspiration questions. What is changing that makes effort worthwhile? Seize the momentum.
- **RAISE the topic of meeting and communication standards.** What should our meeting standards be? How long should meetings be? Does each meeting have a purpose? Confirm who needs to attend and how people should show up. Do this for every meeting or don't hold that meeting. For email or messaging, confirm with

everyone when to include others and other "rules of engagement" that should be followed.

- **RAISE the topic of governance.** It is at this stage that you can move to formal governance. It needn't be boring. What is imperative here is to adopt practical protocols. You could do the same for yourself personally. What are your best habits? Describe them to instill supportive discipline. Take your job description as an individual starting point, but also take Art Ochoa's advice on when and whether to focus on certain parts of your role. If you cannot figure out how to describe governance or specific jobs, the environment is not controlled enough. And, without that control, you and your organization are unlikely to reach higher states of focus.

Level 4: Proactive

To raise the organization to Level 4, the team needs to move from a command-and-control arrangement whereby governance and policies are dogmatic to a team that anticipates needs. Every organization must be reactive at times, but proactive teams not only control what they know but they are ready for what might come. On the technical side, for instance, this means a real and actionable disaster recovery plan is in place. For major gift philanthropy, this means the team has built a robust and long-range pipeline for funding.

With protocols and policies as second nature, these teams have elevated their focus. They have goals that are alive, not just words. The gift administration team, for instance, moves from "gift entry" to "gift analysis" and all team members are encouraged to take initiative. For proactive shops, a few key considerations come to mind:

- **RAISE your prospect touchpoints.** What is the team's POV on touchpoints? Are there enough? Too many? A whole lot of fundraising success comes down to engaging constituents. Really proactive teams thoroughly plan their future work and they stick to those plans. They are persistent. They follow through. Rather than hope for the best, they seek to make the best happen. They record future actions in their databases to remind themselves of these targets.

- **RAISE your overall data strategy.** What is the team's POV on data strategy? How useful is what's being collected? Leverage data. At these levels, your team should trust reports and metrics and have at least a budding predictive analytics program.
- **RAISE your rewards for innovation.** Proactivity is challenging to attain amidst the constant craziness. Even proactive shops are still running in circles at times. Create ways that your team will seek innovations, such as real or quirky awards to recognize innovations. There is a reason it seems every college football team has a "Dog Tagz!" award or professional baseball players get a sizable ring when they win the World Series. Rewards for making the team better motivate team members to do more and go beyond their mere assignments. Being thoughtful about what will motivate your colleagues is a big part of getting everyone to focus on the big picture and stay proactive.

Level 5: Focused

Focused fundraising moves the organization (and individual) from productivity to purpose. It is perhaps uniquely achievable in the nonprofit space because a profit imperative is not the primary driver for the organization's goal. Akin to Urban's return on mission, highly focused organizations are purpose-driven up and down the team. Choices are made based on the ability to serve the mission. In the case of, say, MD Anderson Cancer Center, that means their goal is to put themselves out of business. Eradicating cancer in their case is such a worthwhile cause, organizing around their "why," that their brand displays a slash through the word "Cancer."

Fully mature teams stop doing things, big and small. For instance, that newsletter that had been important to someone years ago and has been maintained as a sign of "being productive" is now recast or cast out. A few tactics that will help you and your team attain focused fundraising:

- **RAISE the topic of organized abandonment.** A phrase coined by Peter Drucker, "organized abandonment" is regularly asking the question "What can we stop doing?" Is this newsletter still needed? How about this annual report? Does it need to be so long? This leads organizations to say "Yes ... and" to keep constituents and stakeholders happy and seek ways to let go of low-yield activities.

- **RAISE the topic of values.** There are too many choices most days, so do the smartest, highest-return things first. You may not be able to work those important things to fruition each day, but you risk mastering the urgent if you are not disciplined in your focus. This is a lesson CASE's Cara Giacomini shared with her "two top items" approach. Establish Blaire Atkinson's "blind trust" that your team can set and then realize its values.

- **RAISE the topic of focus ... regularly.** What is your culture on focus? Too often, projects "just need to get done" at levels that detract from purpose. Instead, authorize the team to delve into the best bets. Allow for self-directed teams to let some things go. Cancel what you do not need to do. Like Ochoa, who trims meeting times on the fly, minimize meetings. Take a hard look at the "solutions" present in social and digital chat tools.

- **RAISE the topic of overhead.** What's the team's POV on overhead? Are you starving yourselves? A constant obstacle to achieving Level 5 maturity is the "low overhead" imperative. Too often, even Level 4 shops find themselves in front of the Board, pitching budget investments, and learning that next year they get to do "more with less." Only slightly less bad is "more with the same," but at least a maturing organization can learn how to maximize its returns from its resources and efforts. To break that cycle, you must start showing why healthier investment from your organization is necessary along with the cost of not investing. Resources, in the form of budget and staff members, should concurrently help you spend more time delivering better fundraising results by cutting through the clutter.

The Focused Fundraising Maturity Model (FFMM) is a road map to better results. If you're honest and fair in your self-appraisal, your natural motivation to improve will kick in. Invite colleagues to share their perspective. The more you discuss focus and where you are in this model, the more likely you are to raise your sights.

20

Further Thoughts on Thought Work

In *2030: How Today's Biggest Trends Will Collide and Reshape the Future of Everything*, Mauro Guillén describes the skills necessary to thrive over the next 10 years.

It isn't yet too late to prepare for 2030. The first, indispensable step is to realize that the world as we know it will irretrievably evanescence at some point during our lifetime, most likely within ten years. This awareness must lead to challenging received wisdom instead of continuing to honor inherited assumptions and ways of thinking. Pursue lateral connections by diversifying your ideas, taking incremental steps, keeping your options open, focusing on opportunity, considering scarcity as an incentive, and riding the tailwinds.

Thought work—the ability to plan, decide, and self-direct—is only going to become more vital at every level of a fundraising organization and in every aspect of fundraising. As more work is automated and is unbounded by time and place, the executive functions of our brain and our ability to sustain thought work are essential. In the remaining pages, we reflect on thought work tips and tricks that can simplify decision-making and improve your focus, and Chapter 21 reflects on a philosophy for sustaining thought work, causativity, which sprang up at Yale as an alternative approach to productivity that incorporates principles of mindfulness.

Train Your Brain

Logical fallacies and biases are important to recognize. Many of us who rose from the social sciences, arts, and humanities to land unexpectedly in this hallowed but unheralded fundraising profession probably had a killer logic class at university, so some of this will be familiar. Mastering these tips and tricks of the brain will give you an advantage in gaining focus and doing meaningful thought work. Some of the most common mental traps include:

- **Ad hominem fallacies** stem from personalizing arguments and strategies in ways irrelevant to the situation. In fundraising, this is a tough one to avoid as so many of our strategies are highly personal, but keep in mind that you are wired to remember negative experiences with people in ways that may allow such ad hominem thinking to cloud your judgment.
- **Straw man arguments**, which are weak starting positions designed to prove your point. "They probably will not answer the phone anyway" is a classic straw man excuse to not make that next prospect call.
- The **false dichotomy fallacy**, a classic problem in fundraising. Too often, we see donors as in or out, with us or not, rather than along a longer continuum allowing for many more positions and choices. Allowing for more nuanced options and holistic considerations will better reflect your reality. This is the reason MIT's Joe Manok keeps those donors who said "no thanks" on his whiteboard; he wants to see when and whether he can re-engage them.
- **Slippery slope** thinking, which also clouds our judgment. This fallacy stems from suggesting that unlikely, often much worse,

outcomes are going to happen if a smaller action is taken. This often takes the form of defeatist thinking about engaging constituents in just the right way. That is, the idea that "if this is not perfect, they will never engage with us" is a prevalent deterrent to taking the first step.

- **Circular arguments** are tautological. Of course. But seriously, this sort of thinking is a big problem in the industry's efforts to optimize analytics. For instance, we often see analytics projects that simply confirm that our best donors are our best donors. Too often, such efforts have endogenous data points that simply reflect what we already know. The number of studies that show that our best future donors are our current donors can become something of a tautology and a self-fulfilling prophecy.

- The **appeal to hypocrisy**, or tu quoque, fallacy is something many of us internalize. "Why should I do my contact reports if Ed doesn't?" is a common manifestation of this way of thinking and it can paralyze good behavior. Set your own focused direction to avoid keeping up with the dot-Joneses or otherwise comparing yourself with the wrong measures.

- The **fallacy of sunk costs** is a classic management-level blunder. That system you set up or those metrics you made everyone record become a thing unto itself. Stopping seems like quitting rather than being the smart move. The same can apply to dropping unresponsive prospects, whereby the fundraiser could gain more time back to use more wisely if only they could let go of that long shot.

- The **appeal to authority fallacy** is a classic problem for fundraisers. Chris sees this first-hand as a consultant from whom people expect guidance and counsel. There are times when counsel is misused, misapplied, or misconstrued for other purposes. The key to avoiding this fallacy is understanding the authority's provenance and credibility for the topic at hand, particularly related to "best practices." In fact, Chris coined the phrase "practices that are best" to remind fundraisers to learn from other authorities but to focus on their unique considerations when building strategies and practices.

There are other tips and tricks to be learned about the brain and its cognition tendencies. A bonus tendency to be mindful of is our brain's negativity bias. Gladwell's *Blink* details the reality that our brain makes snap decisions and generally takes the most negative (read: risk-averse) view. This folds well into other common biases that affect our cognition and focus, such as confirmation bias, which is featured in the Heaths' book *Decisive*.

Be Decisive

The Heath brothers' *Switch* and *Made to Stick* are seminal works in persuasion and change management. In *Decisive*, the authors focus on the "four villains of decision making" (which are narrow framing, confirmation bias, short-term emotion, and overconfidence). Awareness of these villains protects our focus.

Decisive shows a path toward focus that aligns well with the RAISE mantra and the guidance throughout *Focused Fundraising*. Keep options open and avoid confirmation bias. Keeping emotions and confidence in check helps, too. This level of decisiveness leads to better results. You are acting more like CASE's Cara Giacomini or Oklahoma State's Blaire Atkinson. You are pushing big things further along or doing the things that only you can do. Beyond "doing the work" and "hitting your metrics," think about whether those targets are too narrow. Before deciding whether to make that next call or not, consider whether you are reflecting on past performance too heavily, leading to bias, trepidation, and inefficacy. Before you spend the mental energy on getting mad or defensive, choose to take a walk and clear your head. And, when doing so, think of your core cause, your passion, and mission, which will take you further than an action-first mentality.

A final idea in *Decisive* warrants attention because it highlights the challenge of focus in a sea of incessant noise. *Decisive*'s Chapter 3 on "multitracking" highlights what we almost titled this book, "The And Game." In the Heaths' writing, they find power in the idea of replacing "or" with "and." There is a positivity to it. Study after study finds that often both things can be done, so why limit your choices?

This is a great, feel-good notion, until you need to make a split decision, a judgment call, one that will jeopardize your focus. Can you write that proposal and text with your friend? Which is more important? How do you decide? Often you can experience instant overload. Focus is about raising your sights, but remember that it can be okay to multi-task, multi-track, and make friends with distraction *and* focus.

Choices flow naturally with practice. Mihaly Csikszentmihalyi of the University of Chicago coined the term *flow* in 1975 and subsequently wrote *Flow* (1990) and *Finding Flow* (1998) to detail his thinking. Achieving a state of flow suggests that the focused fundraiser is confident in their decisions and actions, and each next step or activity stems seamlessly from the previous one. Sometimes called peak performance or being in "the zone," most of us know what it feels like. The bigger trick is figuring out how to get into a state of flow and then maintain it, despite the distractions that beset us each day. The more topics you RAISE, the more you are able to focus without forcing it. That's flow.

The Value of Heuristics: Big Rocks, Iron Triangles, and Rules of Thumb

Part of simplifying complex thought work comes from heuristics, aka rules of thumb. For example, as a social scientist in graduate school during the 1990s, Chris remains surprised at how often Thucydides's *Peloponnesian Wars* applies to all sorts of circumstances. "Fortune goes to those best prepared" is 2,500-year-old advice that is as true today as in the Mediterranean in 450 BC. For today's thought work, you can put the "big rocks" story at the top of your list.

Big Rocks

What do you do first, the big stuff or the little stuff?

You may remember the following tale of prioritization from Philosophy 101. If you haven't heard it, consider it a key rule of thumb for sequencing tasks. The story goes like this:

Imagine a professor standing in front of a desk. On the desk is a large glass jar, a glass of water, a bowl of sand, some gravel, and a few big rocks. The professor turns to the students: "I need to get these things into this jar. Can you help me?"

Students come to the desk, suggest different options and test different sequences. In some cases, all of the sand fills the glass jar. In others, it was unused. Water is spilled or untouched. Most notably, some of the larger rocks and even some gravel could scarcely be made to fit. After 30 minutes of trial and error, the professor asks the class to take their seats and watch closely. He then shows them how what seemed impossible can be done. First he puts in the largest rocks, then the gravel, then the sand, and then the water. Done. All in. The students are mildly impressed, but some have already jumped ahead to the lesson.

"What did you learn from this?" asks the professor.

"You need to start with the big rocks," they reply in unison.

"And what are the big rocks?" the professor asks further.

"Important stuff, like health, safety, and family," they respond.

"I learned one other important thing," a brave student adds.

"Okay. What's that?" the surprised professor asks.

"You learn faster when someone's already done what you are trying to do."

And so, the focused fundraiser can take two lessons from this:

1. Addressing bigger items first will yield better results. It is critical for focus. Your "big rocks" (including the mission of your institution, your board, top prospects, key programs, and systems and operational resources) need to take first position in your work and thinking.

2. Learning from others' experiences can jump-start your progress. Available resources like RAISE and the Focused Fundraising Maturity Model can play an outsized role in how you and your team develop focus.

Iron Triangles

Big rocks are lasting, but the strongest shape may be the triangle. Following are "iron triangles" sturdy enough to guide most teams.

The "People, Process, Tools" Triangle

Thinking in terms of people, processes, and tools keeps you centered on the big picture. These three elements are de facto components of every fundraising campaign readiness study, every reorganization, and every CRM implementation. For instance, Chris has routinely been called into organizations to evaluate their "tools" (typically, the database, reporting tools, engagement technology, and budget) only to pretty immediately see that, despite owning all of the right tech, "processes" are the root cause of an issue. In one situation on the West Coast, the head of development confidently stated, "We need a new database." In this leader's view, the tools were wrong. However, closer inspection showed that training (people and process) was the culprit. The team had tools, but did not know how to use what they had. This is all too common. For the focused fundraiser, being able to swiftly make better decisions allows more time to focus on Board members and billionaires.

Project Management's Iron Triangle

If you're leading a large project, you can rely on the bedrock triangle of scope, cost, and time. Figure 20.1 presents the simplest form of the Project Management Iron Triangle. The reality is that every project has different sizes, timing, and resource considerations. And you can surely use project management thinking to help with prospect, campaign, and relationship management strategies and focus.

The project management triangle keeps you honest about trade-offs. If you want to finish something quicker, there are costs. If you want to increase scope (do more), it needs more time. Viewing work—including prospecting, programs, campaigns—through the project management lens with the scope-cost-time triangle will generally help clarify the moving parts and allow better decisions and focus as a result.

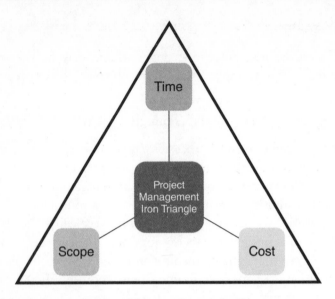

Figure 20.1   Scope, Cost, and Time as Levers for Focus

Fundraising Operations Triangle

In *An Executive's Guide to Fundraising Operations*, Chris showed the trade-offs in fundraising operations with the accuracy, speed, and volume triangle. Designed with the fundraising executive in mind, it helps think through high-volume processes. In particular, professionals have three levers to pull to address quality outcomes (such as better data, accurate materials, and happier donors). For example, nonprofits in the United States receive an average of over 33% of their gift volume from Thanksgiving to New Year's Day. So, that is one-third of all giving volume is generally received in about one-tenth of a year. Hence, volume is high during a time that the team is likely very engaged in family and personal activities compared to other times of year. What is a leader to do? In general, you can either hire more help, work through the piles with the same folks, or be less picky about the entry of some gifts. Where these blips are routine and expected, you may also look at automation or overall policy change. Perhaps a caging company can handle some lockbox volume (and, if you do not yet have a lockbox, maybe you need to get one).

How can lockboxes and gift caging help you focus? Merkle Response Management Group's Kent Grove, president, and Amy Bobrick, vice president, have been helping organizations figure this out for years. Merkle RMG is a top operational support and caging company. In short, they process the end-to-end activity to process millions of gifts for hundreds of clients. These two know about handling high volume. In an interview with Chris, they shared a few central ideas that allow for their services to balance out advancement services shops. To start, Merkle RMG has a thorough onboarding process. They ask many, many questions and attempt to get the workflow right. Second, they tie into the USPS and FedEx/UPS mail stream, as well as serve as a lockbox clearinghouse for clients' online and mobile giving. Once checks and digital gifts arrive for Merkle RMG to process, they go through a series of high-volume handling and exception management steps. The arrangement is clever and has good controls. In some cases, the Merkle RMG team enters gifts and pledges directly into their clients' databases. Like others in this space, they have thought of nearly everything, and they have an exception management team to handle unexpected items. As Kent shared during the discussion: "We see ourselves as an extension of our clients. This means we treat their donors with the attention they would." This is the focus, layered into a solid business process and technical environment, that has allowed Merkle RMG to help its clients grow.

Now, nothing has distracted more fundraisers than the idea of "greater inaccuracy." From angry donor calls to angry donor policies, one small $50 error can sometimes distract a whole team for weeks or more. But should it? Can you get to a place where you allow the little stuff to roll off of your back? Where the sand and water cannot quite fit in the glass jar but you have the big rocks covered? Absolutely! In fact, that is what focused fundraising is about. Fix the systemic. Address the monumental. Don't sweat the small stuff. Avoid anecdotal outcomes driving policy. These lessons from this heuristic can save your team hours and energy that you can pour into major and principal giving.

The 80/20 Rule

The 80/20 rule, or Pareto principle, is a heuristic with such wide applicability you hear it in nearly every field. For focused fundraising, it's valuable to keep in mind.

Vilfredo Pareto was a polymath whose ideas are eminently applicable to fundraising. He illustrated that choices between two things (like major donors and annual donors) fall along a curve between having none of one and an overabundance of the other or, optimally, the right number of each. His thinking established a way of visualizing choices (Pareto charts), which codified the notion of "marginal return." Marginal returns are looking for the 1,001st annual donor at the expense of any major donors.

Pareto's most important contribution to aid focused fundraising is the Pareto principle, aka the 80/20 rule. He observed (in the 1800s, by the way ... boy, did these guys have a lot of time to think and focus back then before all those distractions on our iPhones and TV!) that 80% of productivity comes from 20% of resources. For fundraising, especially in sophisticated major giving shops, this means that a small percentage of donors will give a high percentage of contributions over a year or a campaign. The CASE 2010 Campaign Study found that about 93% of all higher education giving comes from the top 10% of campaign gifts. A vice president for advancement at an ACC school told Chris in October 2021 that 97% of his multibillion-dollar campaign was funded by 3% of his donors. In one momentous year for an East Coast university that raised over $500 million in a single year, the numbers were more like 99%-to-1%, whereby one donor's $100 million-plus gift added to the generosity of a few other mega- and major-donor contributions to account for nearly all of the organization's giving that year.

How can the 80/20 rule work for you? Remember that your greatest results often come from a small percentage of your prospects. Put 20% on the front burner and keep the 80% on simmer. At every organization, someone has to work smaller and smaller capacity prospects. Principal giving, then major, then annual giving efforts all have a "bottom" that, generally, amount to smaller donations. The Focused Fundraising Maturity Model is built with the 80/20 principle in mind. Let's now turn to the Golden Rule.

The Golden Rule(s)

Many of us grew up knowing the Golden Rule as "Do unto others as you would have them do to you." Basically, "Be nice," right? This is a spectacularly important principle to follow. It is one of those "everything I ever needed to learn I learned in kindergarten" maxims. And most in fundraising are good at this one, but sometimes to our peril.

How could being nice be a bad thing? David Dunlop's 1987 CASE *Currents* article highlights the math. His article spawned the notion of "moves management," which illustrated that a fundraiser typically has under 1,000 hours a year to cultivate and solicit donors. Gladwell's *Tipping Point* analysis already showed us that the brain can only handle so many relationships. Put these two together and every long lunch with a mid-level donor with three kids still in college, nine grandkids already, and a list of nonprofits on the list ahead of yours is eating into your impact. This stinks, but it is true. Top performers have a way of either making the most of their time or, workaholic-style, working more. The notion of saying no or using "yes, and ..." can be much more palatable to fundraising professionals to use their time for the most impact.

An alternative, classic fundraising Golden Rule is that "they who have the gold makes the rules." This somewhat harsh viewpoint is a reality for many principal giving efforts. These days, sometimes 100–200 people in America account for 10% or more of every dollar given to charity. An organization's mission should not bend uncontrollably to the whims of such donors; our constituents and our society deserve more than that. However, really focused fundraisers often succeed because they treat their best chances as their big rocks. And this can be hard.

Now, we do not ascribe to life as a zero-sum game nor seek to reinforce social injustices. There is merit in meeting, no matter the potential naming opportunities that person may select in the next campaign. And, as the "do unto others" version of the rule implies, a blanket "be nice" policy may help you identify surprising prospects. There are opportunities everywhere and you need to be looking for them—just maybe do not keep looking after the third lunch.

Practicing Rules of Thumb

Dozens of professionals just like you have sharpened focused fundraising. You have learned about Art Ochoa and Blaire Atkinson's respective advice—do your top few things and have those be the things only you can do. Interviews with fundraising professionals hammered home the utility of basic rules of thumb such as the ones we've discussed. As an example of an iron triangle in practice, let's turn to Dwight Dozier.

Dwight Dozier is Georgia Tech Foundation's CIO. He is seasoned and deeply skilled via a long-tenured career including stints with Washington State University, Penn State University, George Washington University, and the University of Louisville. He serves as a Board member for the Association of Advancement Services Professionals and recently served as chair of the Blackbaud CRM Higher Education Product Advisory Group. Even with his extensive background, he encountered new challenges in Georgia Tech's pursuit and implementation of a new CRM. These sorts of projects are monsters. He has slayed such dragons in past roles but with less complicated and flexible features. Colleagues rightfully wanted every customization and configuration up front to support their work. But just because they had this expectation did not mean Dwight could be expected to deliver this at the onset. So, in real time, day after day, he applied the project management iron triangle. If and as new ideas were added, he asked what could be pushed or removed from scope. He was master of the "yes, and ...," whereby the team successfully launched on time, yet purposefully planned a year post-implementation to "achieve operational parity" in most areas with additional planned work for enhancements. He would deftly wield the "people, process, tool" heuristic to organize efforts and manage time and work realities. In short, seeing Dwight over a 36-month period illustrated the value of using these heuristics to contain the multitudinous distractions that a CRM implementation will bring.

As Dozier explained during a recent podcast with Chris, managing the important with the urgent is always a challenge. Dozier shared: "People are coming forward with bright new ideas, newly equipped with all of this new potential while we still need to manage the standard work and data. Managing the day-to-day while creating a road map and vision of expectations 10 years out of where we want to be and should be is exciting, but we must manage those expectations." Dozier also indicated it was important to manage on "the customer's side with the 'Wow!' moments leading to managing the 'Can't you just' requests," which can require hundreds of hours of work. "This 'just' word can be dangerous and there is excitement behind that word, too." In managing the environment and expectations, he is clear that his team has made significant progress but is "still evolving." Like a focused fundraiser, Dozier can see that the future is an "evolving space where we are ever in pursuit of being where our constituents are." To keep up, like all of us, he will need to deftly manage distractions, overcome overload, and apply a focus-first approach.

21

Causativity

None of us is an inexhaustible resource.
—Umi Howard, senior director, McNulty Leadership Program,
Wharton School, University of Pennsylvania

NONE OF US can go 24/7 like the devices we use. We use tech words like "bandwidth" and "processing" to describe our mental life, as though a quick "recharge" can keep us humming along like the electric grid and our battery-powered creations. But there is nothing about us that is inexhaustible. Our minds are wonderfully human, and our focus and thought are delightfully embodied.

So how do we sustain focused thought work, day after day?

Thought work—planning, deciding, considering, remembering—requires self-direction. But in a world pulsing with the 4 Ms—constant messages, back-to-back meetings, always-updated media, and ever-changing management metrics—it's easy to exhaust our faculties. To make it more challenging, the bar for self-direction and focused thought work keeps getting higher. How many fundraising jobs in your shop require a "self-starter"? How many of us can be self-starters 100% of the time?

The concept of causativity emerged among Yale staff during the pandemic. Yale University is the proud home of the Yale Center for Emotional Intelligence, the Yale Stress Center, and, recently, The Good Life Center. At Yale, emotional intelligence and civic responsibility are in the culture. Drawing on the culture, the academic leaders, and in conjunction with outside leaders in coaching, mindfulness, and productivity, causativity became a way to describe an emerging trend: alternative approaches to productivity that incorporate mindfulness. Rather than viewing mindfulness as something you do to recover from work or enhance your work, you view it as an essential part of being the one doing all that work. You are a person first and a worker second. One of the early pioneers of causativity, Meredith Fahey, an organizational effectiveness expert and marvelous human being, gave causativity shape and meaning with the phrase "always keep an eye on why."

Does the world need another buzzword? We see causativity as more than that. To be causative is to work mindfully. Life's too short to be reactive all the time. We can all be pinball workers and we can be intentional human beings. But given the tech tug, the 4 Ms, and instant overload, we need supports to be causative. Focused fundraising supports thought work by emphasizing the value of perspective and clarity of standards. RAISE is meant to help you sustain thought work by engaging your full faculties more deeply. Each time you RAISE a topic and set a focused direction, you access emotional intelligence as well as your intellect. With every topic you RAISE, where you settle your POV, and assess your standards, you access a level of focus that steadies and empowers by honoring the fullness of your experience. A focused direction depends on having more than your head in it— your heart and your body need to be there, too. And when you are fully there, your mind can rest.

Nonprofit life is driven by empathy. The corporate sector tries to imitate nonprofit values with "corporate social responsibility" campaigns, but the nonprofit sector lives and breathes these values every day. Nonprofits exist for the public good, not for private purposes. Because of the beating heart in them, nonprofits really do rely on self-starters and self-direction. So, it is especially important to have an overarching philosophy that values us as people first and workers second. Empathy is what sustains meaning for an organization and for an individual. Insight is what makes it possible to say "enough is enough." Clarity of empathy and insight is what makes us say, "I've done my very best."

In his chapter in *Invisible Labor: Hidden Work in the Contemporary World*, John W. Budd points out the relationship between work and meaning. He asserts a profound philosophical belief: "Self-directed work is the essential quality of being human." Self-directed work is also what leading management thinker Peter Drucker foresaw when he gazed into the twenty-first century and theorized about technology, our future, and the future of our sector. We are at the beginning of a sea change in work and nonprofit life. To realize the meaning in the constant craziness, in all our fundraising efforts, we need to sustain all of our good thinking. We need our minds and bodies to support self-direction, and we need to lean on each other. As focused individuals and organizations, we can RAISE our sights and become a little more causative each day.

Conclusion

THROUGHOUT *FOCUSED FUNDRAISING*, you have met leaders in the field who rise above the noise. Consider Joe Manok, who kept his team going in unimaginable circumstances. In our interview about Joe's focus on principal giving at MIT, you learned of an agile professional who prioritized and calibrated his efforts, went into discussions to listen and learn, and exhibited consistent authenticity about the real reasons for his work—his donor's passion for the mission he served. When he started his career in 2006, Joe balanced different challenges. This expert fundraiser at MIT was once a gift processor on the campus of American University of Beirut in Lebanon. During the brief but traumatic war between Hezbollah and Israel, Joe did something that required amazing focus. While bombs dropped and tensions flared, he made sure AUB could keep processing gifts. He also made sure they could keep soliciting gifts for their medical school's efforts to tend to those wounded and affected by that war. Joe's focus allowed him and his colleagues to keep going. Like Joe's decision to do the next right thing for AUB, your choice—to set a focused direction for yourself and your team—really matters.

To raise your sights and overcome overload, you have everything you need. Focused fundraising is not the secret to magically "do it all." Rather, it's about valuing all you do, especially, in Atkinson's words, "only those things only you can do." None of us is perfectly focused, so with a mission you care about you have a starting point to strengthen your focus every day. The following reminders reiterate how you and your organization can achieve focus for lasting relationships and financial support.

Key Reminders Toward Focused Fundraising

There have been some important themes that will guide you.

- **Focus**—Focus is not about narrowing attention; it is about zooming out and zooming in as appropriate. It's knowing why something matters to you and setting a direction you are likely to follow.
- **Fundraising**—Fundraising is not just about enthusiasm and raising money. Fundraising is a thoughtful discipline, an art and science that requires focused thought work to consistently deliver results.
- **Distraction**—Distractions serve as a reminder that focus has been diverted. Even the most minor distractions can reveal open questions about what matters to you and how you can set a direction you can follow.
- **Focus-first versus action-first**—Focus-first means to set direction before you act. Action-first is generally reactive and frequently contributes to overload.
- **Tech tug**—The yanking on our attention from tech, at the organizational and personal levels.
- **The 4 Ms**—Messages, meetings, media, and management—the common sources of overload.
- **Instant overload**—What leads to distraction because you forget what you're doing (like opening your inbox to see what someone wrote and spotting three other messages first, or opening your browser only to discover 14 open tabs you'd forgotten).
- **Multi-tasking on purpose**—Multi-tasking is not distracting unless it's multi-purposing. If you're multi-tasking on purpose, you might be fine. For example, being in a meeting and googling something that comes up is not multi-purposing—it is multi-tasking on purpose.

- **Maturity models**—Whether for major giving, focused fundraising, or some other purpose, maturity models give you a way to visualize a continuum that requires earlier stages to build to greater outcomes.
- **Causativity**—An alternative approach to productivity that incorporates principles of mindfulness. We all know we can be productive and go nowhere (check menial tasks off the list) and we can be on purpose and go nowhere (dreaming about writing a novel, but not writing). The art of purposeful thought work is to be causative.

On a daily basis you have a chance to practice a focus-first mentality and create focus-friendly practices. Handling the 4 Ms is the training ground. Keep in mind that it's a process—no one has it all mastered.

- **Messages**—Before checking your phone, ask yourself why. Why check now? Is there something specific you are looking for? Or is it just a vague need to check? When reading a message, ask yourself what it means before deciding what to do about it. Separate reading and replying so you write intentionally. That's focus-first.
- **Meetings**—Before deciding to meet or not to meet, ask yourself what purpose the meeting serves. Is it likely to serve that purpose? Is it likely not to? If not, how do you relate to it? Can you ask at the end of the meeting, as a result of this meeting, where are we now? That's focus-first.
- **Media**—Before opening to news or updates, ask yourself why. To learn? To read? See what's happening with others? That's focus-first.
- **Management**—Before taking action on an issue, understand what purpose the action might serve. Review and question your metrics. Learn to ask respectfully and with context. RAISE topics yourself and then question them with others. That's focus-first.

We hope that the journey that we have been on together has given you solid ground for turning the constant craziness of nonprofit life into a rewarding, fun, and exciting challenge. We hope you feel inspired to use RAISE frequently in order to elevate focus for yourself and those around you. As you apply RAISE, we are confident you can rely on your self-reflection as your best guide.

- **Train your brain.** Realizing the primordial and instinctual hurdles you are up against is an important step to attaining focus. Pings and dings get our attention for reasons you are not powerless to overcome. The best offense here is a good understanding of how you work, what works for you, and becoming mindful of the ways you can be most focused.
- **Spin the spinning top.** Most professionals do not expect a Luddite turn away from digital distractions anytime soon. Our research showed that professionals felt like they are more distracted than ever. It is better to be the spinner than be spun; you can do this by consistently applying RAISE to situations you face.
- **Practice what is best.** Every nonprofit professional and volunteer is different and so this book's treatment of issues and ideas will affect each of you differently. There is no absolute playbook for dealing with the constant craziness and establishing the focus you need. Your best bet is to reflect and learn from your experiences.

Most of all, RAISE your focus. Use RAISE—recognize your POV, assess your standards, inspire your efforts, structure your work, and evolve your approach—for topics large and small so that it becomes a habit. Whenever you recognize your point of view, you stand on firmer ground. When you assess your standards, you make completion possible. When you inspire your efforts, you seize all the momentum you can. When you structure your work, you gain control. And, finally, when you evolve your approach, you proceed with an open mind. Amidst the daily digital distractions we all face, knowing how to set focused direction for yourself and others is perhaps the most important skill in the twenty-first century.

As a nonprofit professional or volunteer, you have what it takes to help you and your team focus. The mindset that wins donors and dollars also wins over distraction. You can structure your daily work and your organization's processes to support focus. You can use mindfulness to turn distraction into focus, one tech tug at a time. We wish you every success in all your nonprofit endeavors …

Discussion Questions

You and your team will benefit from thinking about and discussing focus. Remember, focus doesn't just happen. These questions will prompt you to remember lessons from the book and apply your thinking to whatever important challenges you face.

Constant Craziness

- Do you describe your life as "crazy" or "crazy busy"? How come?
- Would you describe working at your organization as crazy? Sometimes? All the time?
- What do you think contributes to the constant craziness?

Tech Tug

- How does the organizational tech tug—the lure of new tech—play out in your organization?
- How does the personal tech tug impact your culture? In meetings? Off-hours?
- What protocols do you keep or does your organization keep to address the tech tug?

Instant Overload

- When do you notice instant overload most? In the morning? After lunch? At the end of the day?
- Which of the 4 Ms is the greatest contributor to instant overload? Messages? Media? Meetings? Management? Why do you think that is the case?
- How does instant overload affect your organization?

Focused Fundraising

- Where do you see your organization on the Focused Fundraising Maturity Model? How come?
- What are the greatest challenges to attaining focus at your organization?
- What is your culture of valuing fundraising? How valuable is time spent on fundraising compared to other activities?

Toolkit: RAISE: Practical Examples and Coaching Prompts

RAISE IS MEANT to elevate focus. It takes you through the five phases to set a focused direction. A focused direction is one you're likely to follow. You can apply RAISE to any topic. The following two examples help you think through the application of RAISE to improve your focus.

1. Recognize your point of view (POV).
2. Assess your standards.
3. Inspire your efforts.
4. Structure your work.
5. Evolve your approach.

Topic #1: Merger or Partner with Another Organization?

Although commonplace in the for-profit sector, mergers can be viewed as a third rail for many nonprofit Boards. If you serve on a Board that struggles to raise money, or if you're part of a larger organization that's underperforming, and you read *Focused Fundraising* in the hope that it would cure that, we hope you found the answers you were looking for. However, if you are still wondering if your organization can go it alone, then you might want to check out this thought exercise on mergers and partnerships using the RAISE framework.

The potential for mergers and acquisitions is a touchy subject, but the merits are too hard to ignore. The ultimate confirmation bias in our industry is that our organizations are needed as they currently exist. Why shouldn't you be open to combining with another organization with a similar mission? Let's RAISE this tricky topic.

Recognize Your Point of View

- Who are the "they" in this situation and what are they looking for? Often partner organizations are ones you know well. Perhaps it is an organization you've worked with in the past.
- Who is the "we" and what are we after? Perhaps it is you and a few other Board members who have lightly discussed it.
- What is the "it," and what is its role? In this case it could be a merger or a partnership or some other kind of arrangement. There are countless different kinds of arrangements.
- Finally, where am I on this topic? Perhaps you have been discussing it casually but you're ready to have a more serious talk about it.

Assess Your Standards

- What standards are you using? You see other organizations that seem to have a more solid foundation. You don't want to be panicked about funding the budget year after year.

Inspire Your Efforts

- What is changing that makes the effort worthwhile? You've seen a real shift in the Board and you know others are intrigued by the possibility. The conversation has come up several times at meetings.

Structure Your Work

- What plans or commitments are you holding? You know you want to do due diligence. You want to reality check by looking at comparable organizations' 990s.

Evolve Your Approach

- Given the thought, where are you now? You are ready to talk it over with the Board chair, and propose that a portion of the next meeting be devoted to this topic.

This example is intended to simplify a complex subject. Chris has lately been a part of setting strategy with a substantial number of merging shops, largely in the health care space. While there is work involved in making these happen, a "one CRM" approach where there was once an "X separate databases" approach saves money, streamlines operations, improves reporting and analytics capacity, and generally helps your organization mature in focus and in results. So, if you did see even a glimmer of opportunity, explore it. Imagine what double the people could accomplish. Imagine what shared services models might allow for vis-à-vis economies of scale.

As another quick example of the value proposition of merging shops, when studying the ratio of prospect research officer to gift officers, groups like APRA, the authority on prospect development, tend to suggest a ratio of 1 prospect professional to 4 or so gift officers. But this is a reflection of statistical bias in the form of a Poisson distribution (i.e., having 1 researcher is more common and no organization has −1 researcher). When you examine the prospecting teams of very large shops, the ratio gets closer to 1 to 10. The benefits of two merging nonprofits will be in closer alignment with how bigger teams are structured and, as a result, how much more money bigger teams raise.

The resounding message here is that, even for a very complex, distracting, and overwhelming topic, if you RAISE the topic you can surface new insights.

Topic #2: A New Board Member Aims for More Individual Donations

Let's take a common example that small nonprofits often face. For many nonprofits, there is no full-time development director to drive fundraising activities. Fundraising is up to the Board of directors. And for many Board members, fundraising is last on their list. But Kyra Howard has recently joined this particular Board. Kyra has brought a lot of energy and enthusiasm for the organization and its mission. She has also brought focus. Because Kyra is a composite of volunteer fundraisers and Board members, her RAISE results are illustrative.

Kyra's topic is "individual donors." Every year the Board wants more donations from private individuals. Grants and government funds are hard to get and dwindling. Events are expensive to run. And the organization has always received some donations from private individuals. Why can't they get more? Why can't they sustain it?

Recognize Your Point of View

How am I viewing this topic now? How are others viewing it? Kyra asked herself.

- **Them:** Kyra determined that, in this case, "they" are the dozens of individual donors who have given to the organization over the years. Initially she thought "they" were her other Board members because she did not feel close to them. However, after thinking about it, she concluded that her fellow Board members belong alongside her.
- **Us:** Kyra realized that "we" are the Board. Initially this was a challenge because she felt that the Board seemed to shoot down her ideas and oppose her point of view. But when she stopped and thought about it further, she realized that the whole Board really does want the same thing.
- **It.** Kyra had to think about this for a minute, but then quickly realized what "it" referred to. In this case, she realized that it was the fundraising plan for the year, or rather the lack thereof. There seemed to be no plan—at least not that anyone had ever written down or mentioned.
- **Me:** After a few minutes of reflection, Kyra realized that she wanted to ask the Board members to each do something individually. It was clear to her that her fellow Board members did not really understand or appreciate fundraising. Rather than pitching ideas as she had been doing, she needed to change course.

Assess Your Standards

What standards am I choosing? Kyra asked herself.

One observation that became obvious to Kyra was that she was holding her Board members to a higher standard than was fair. Had any of them ever had fundraising training before? Did they understand what she was talking about? Even though they all recognized the need to raise money, did they understand about cultivation and stewardship? She decided that a more fair standard for her fellow Board members would be to assume they are coming to it with no prior experience, just like she did when she first got involved.

Additionally, she thought her Board members' standards for how much could be raised from individuals in a year was wishful thinking. How could they raise $200,000 this year when there was only $20,000 last year? Perhaps it was possible, but it did not seem realistic. Instead, she decided for herself that a standard would be last year's results plus 10%. Although incremental, and perhaps not tremendously exciting, she did not think 10X growth would be possible in one year, especially with a Board that had no real experience. Perhaps in a few years, if she and others set realistic goals and really worked at them, they could get there.

With greater clarity of roles and standards, a general direction was starting to emerge to Kyra. But rather than writing it out or speaking it at that point, she elected to continue on with the RAISE process.

Inspire Your Efforts

What is changing that makes effort worthwhile? Kyra asked herself next.

There's nothing Kyra likes less than wasting her time and energy. With her kids and her full-time job, she doesn't have a lot of time to spare. So this question was right on point for her. What *is* changing? she asked herself.

There were a few things that came to mind. First, there was one key ally that she had on the Board. In her most recent conversation with T.J., Kyra saw that T.J. was getting it. She's not quite sure what T.J.'s background was but she made a mental note to learn more. Second, she did value all the data the organization had. The staff had done a good job of keeping track of donors from previous years. They were able to give the information to her pretty quickly. And if she asked questions she was able to get answers to them. It wasn't like she had no data to work with at all. And finally, there were a dozen or so donors who had given repeatedly over the years. That probably was enough to build from, if they got focused on it.

A few more possibilities sprang to mind. But Kyra, determined to have focused direction, rather than just bursting into things as she usually did, wanted to complete the RAISE process. So she continued on to the next step.

Structure Your Work

What structures support the work? Kyra asked herself.

Tempting as it was to call the organization a mess and to bemoan the lack of structure, she did have to come back to the fact that there was a donor list. A donor list was good. The problem was commitments— what set structures did the organization already have? She had to think about that one for a moment.

The organization did send appeals every few months …

It did run an event usually once per year …

But what else?

She realized the big missing piece was that there was no structure around stewardship or cultivation. When would donors hear from the organization except for the appeals and the event invitation? How did they know they mattered or their gifts were valued? Had they ever met a Board member?

And then she remembered, *we do have some pretty good year-end reports on our program outcomes.*

A few more assets came to mind as she considered this question and she considered the structures. She became a little clearer on what a focused direction for herself and for her peers on the Board might look like. So she went to the final step of the RAISE process.

Evolve Your Approach

As a result of this process, where am I now on this topic? Kyra asked herself.

As she reflected on this topic, she took a deep breath. The hardest part of moving on is always letting go. She had to let go of the irritation with some of the Board members. She had T.J., who she knew could help get through to some of the others on being more realistic and less demanding. She also had to let go of her own resentment that the organization was in this shape. What did they do before she joined? How had anything gotten done? She had been banging her head against the wall trying to get the Board to understand big-picture ideas, and now she was going to try a different approach. A focused approach. Was it guaranteed to work out? No. But Kyra was fine with that. What she had been doing wasn't going anywhere.

She set a focused direction for herself: *I will talk to T.J. and ask him to look over the donor list with me. We will pick out a few names each and reach out to those people. We will ask them about why they care about the organization and why they've supported it over the years. And then we'll report back to the Board. At that time we'll ask them to choose a few names too. Then T.J. and I can talk to them together about some more realistic goals …*

With this thought in mind, Kyra had a focused direction for herself. Her plan wasn't completely mapped out. She hadn't yet scheduled time with T.J. She didn't have everything all written down. She didn't know if the donors would respond or not. She did not know if her plan would yield fruit. She didn't know if the Board members would agree with her. But she felt confident in this direction because it made sense to her and it felt right. And for Kyra, that was a pretty good test of a focused direction. She knew inside she was likely to stick with it.

RAISE Prompts for Self-Coaching

To RAISE topics that matter to you, try these prompts. It's not important to answer each question, nor to write out your answers. Your goal is to coach yourself in a way that challenges you but is not overwhelming. RAISE fosters a habit of zooming out in order to zoom back in. That's how you focus without forcing it. You do not need to have all the answers on a topic before you start taking action. You may wish to reflect on a few questions, take action, then come back to the topic. Trust your judgment. It's a victory to simply state a topic and attempt to coach yourself with a process like RAISE. You will know you've got a focused direction when you are confident you will follow it.

Topic:

Recognize Your Point of View (POV)

- Who else has a POV on this topic besides me?*
- What is their POV likely to be?
- What is my POV?

Assess Your Standards

- How might I judge success on this topic?
- Who else's standards apply?
- How can I make the standards fair and shared?

Inspire Your Efforts

- Where are the bright spots?
- What is changing that makes effort worthwhile?
- How might I redirect from "No" to "Yes, if …" or "Yes, and …?"

---

*Consider the four perspectives: Us, Them, It, and I. Rather than just considering specific people, it's important to consider teams or groups. Questions on POV can be challenging, so put forward your best guess. It's less important to be right than it is to venture a guess. You can always see by direct experience if your hunches prove to be true.

Structure Your Work

- What supports do I need?
- Who can help add healthy structure?
- What structures are already in place?

Evolve Your Approach

- Where am I now?
- What have I learned?
- How has my POV evolved?

RAISE Prompts for Facilitators

As a team leader or facilitator, you have the opportunity to form a focused direction together. To RAISE topics with your team, you can use these prompts as a backdrop. You can go step-by-step through the questions or you can reflect on them as a whole. Similar to self-coaching, it's not necessary to answer every question in order to focus. You may wish to answer a few, then take action and regroup after the situation has changed.

Topic:

Recognize Your Team's Point of View (POV)

- What is our POV on this topic?*
- Who else do you think has a POV on this besides our team?
- What is our POV as a team?

Assess Your Team Standards

- How might we determine we've been successful on this topic?
- How can we make our standards clear and shared?
- Who else may have relevant standards we can use?

Inspire Your Team Efforts

- Where are our bright spots?
- What is changing that makes our efforts worthwhile?
- How might we redirect from resisting *against* to advocating *for*?

Structure Your Team's Work

- What supports do we need?
- Who can help us add healthy structure?
- What structures do we already have in place?

---

*Consider the four perspectives: Us, Them, It, and I. Each member of the team has their own POV. To encourage diversity of views, listen closely before attempting to state a team POV. It may take several discussions to have a common POV depending on the team size. Although it may take up-front energy, it pays for itself later when you avoid dead ends, resistance, distraction, and a host of other sidetracks.

Evolve Your Team's Approach

- Where are we now?
- What have we learned?
- How has our POV evolved?

RAISE Prompts for Peer Coaching

When a coworker comes to you with a topic, you want to be able to help them set a focused direction. To provide peer coaching with RAISE, the typical coaching advice applies: listen closely and reflect back often. Assume that the best solutions emerge; you're not there to solve a problem, but rather be a sounding board for the other person to arrive at their own solution.

As with the individual and team applications, for peer coaching it's not necessary to state each question aloud and answer each one. Rather, you may wish to talk about just the first few and then your peer may have an idea and want to take action. That's fine. The purpose is to set focused direction, not to have all the answers before you take action.

Topic:

Recognize Their Point of View (POV)
- What is your POV on this topic?*
- Who else do you think has a POV on this besides you?
- What is your POV as a team?

Assess Their Standards
- How might you judge success on this topic?
- How can your standards be known and shared by others?
- Who else may have relevant standards you can use?

Inspire Their Efforts
- Where do you see bright spots?
- What is changing that makes your efforts worthwhile?
- How might you save your energy from being *against* to being *for*?

---

*Consider the four perspectives: Us, Them, It, and I. When you are coaching someone else, it's often necessary to help them widen their POV. Often the other person will be giving attention to a POV they are against, typically a manager or difficult coworker. In order to help them recognize their POV, you can help them reflect broadly on the situation. In that process, they often see new possibilities.

Structure Their Work

- What supports would you find most helpful?
- Who can help you add healthy structure?
- What structures do you already have in place?

Evolve Their Approach

- Where are you now on this topic?
- What have you learned?
- How has your POV evolved?

Bibliography

Allen, David. *Getting Things Done: The Art of Stress-Free Productivity.* Penguin Books, 2003.

Barker, Eric. *Barking Up the Wrong Tree: The Surprising Science Behind Why Everything You Know About Success Is (Mostly) Wrong.* HarperOne, 2017.

Brackett, Hawken. *An Ethical Becoming for Senior Student Affairs Officers: Phronetic Leadership.* University of Alabama, 2018.

Budd, John W. "The Eye Sees What the Mind Knows: The Conceptual Foundations of Invisible Work." In *Invisible Labor: Hidden Work in the Contemporary World*, edited by Marion G. Crain, Winifred R. Poster, and Miriam A. Cherry. University of California Press, 2016.

Cannon, Christopher M. *An Executive's Guide to Fundraising Operations: Principles, Tools and Trends.* Wiley, 2011.

Collins, Jim. *Good to Great: Why Some Companies Make the Leap ... and Others Don't.* HarperBusiness, 2001.

Compernolle, Theo. *BrainChains: Discover Your Brain and Unleash Its Full Potential in a Hyperconnected Multitasking World.* Compublications, 2014.

Cooper, Gabe, and Mckenna Bailey. *Responsive Fundraising: The Donor-Centric Framework Helping Today's Leading Nonprofits Grow Giving.* Liberalis, 2020.

Crain, Marion G., Winifred R. Poster, and Miriam A. Cherry, editors. *Invisible Labor: Hidden Work in the Contemporary World.* University of California Press, 2016.

Crawford, Matthew B. *The World Beyond Your Head: On Becoming an Individual in an Age of Distraction.* Farrar, Straus and Giroux, 2015.

Crum, Alia, and Thomas Crum. "Stress Can Be a Good Thing If You Know How to Use It." *Harvard Business Review,* September 3, 2015.

Csikszentmihalyi, Mihaly. *Flow: The Psychology of Optimal Experience.* Harper Perennial, 1990.

Csikszentmihalyi, Mihaly. *Finding Flow: The Psychology of Engagement with Everyday Life.* Basic Books, 1997.

Dillon, Jay Le Roux, "Factors and Characteristics of Alumni Role Identity: Implications for Practice in Higher Education Fundraising and Alumni Relations." Doctoral dissertations, University of San Francisco. https://repository.usfca.edu/diss/337.

Dunlop, D. R. "The Ultimate Gift." CASE *Currents,* May 1987 (pp. 8–13).

Fine, Alan, and Rebecca R. Merrill. *You Already Know How to Be Great: A Simple Way to Remove Interference and Unlock Your Greatest Potential.* Portfolio Penguin, 2010.

Gallwey, W. Timothy. *The Inner Game of Tennis.* Random House, 1974.

Gladwell, Malcolm. *The Tipping Point: How Little Things Can Make a Big Difference.* Back Bay Books, 2002.

Gladwell, Malcolm. *Blink: The Power of Thinking Without Thinking.* Back Bay Books, 2005.

Gregory, Ann Goggins, and Don Howard. "The Nonprofit Starvation Cycle." *Stanford Social Innovation Review,* Fall 2009.

Guillén, Mauro F. *2030: How Today's Biggest Trends Will Collide and Reshape the Future of Everything.* St. Martin's Press, 2020.

Harari, Yuval Noah. *Sapiens: A Brief History of Humankind.* HarperCollins, 2015.

Harvard Business Review. *HBR's 10 Must Reads: On Mental Toughness (With Bonus Interview of "Post-Traumatic Growth and Building Resilience" with Martin E.P. Seligman).* Harvard Business Review Press, 2018.

Hasseltine, Donald A. "Performance Management Maturity Model: Raising the Bar of Fundraising Performance." CASE white paper, 2010.

Heath, Chip, and Dan Heath. *Decisive: How to Make Better Choices in Life and Work.* Currency, 2013.

Heath, Chip, and Dan Heath. *Made to Stick: Why Some Ideas Survive and Others Die.* Random House, 2008.

Heath, Chip, and Dan Heath. *Switch: How to Change Things When Change Is Hard.* Broadway Books, 2010.

Hirschman, Albert O. *Exit, Voice, and Loyalty: Responses to Decline in Firms, Organizations, and States.* Harvard University Press, 1970.

Johnson, Spencer. *Who Moved My Cheese? An Amazing Way to Deal with Change in Your Work and in Your Life.* G.P. Putnam's Sons, 1988.

Kabat-Zinn, Jon. *Full Catastrophe Living: Using the Wisdom of Your Body and Mind to Face Stress, Pain, and Illness.* Delta Trade Paperbacks, 2005.

Kahneman, Daniel. "Bias Is a Big Problem. But So Is Noise." Guest Essay, *New York Times*, May 15, 2021.

Kahneman, Daniel. *Thinking, Fast and Slow.* Farrar, Straus and Giroux, 2013.

Kahneman, Daniel, Olivier Sibony, and Cass R. Sunstein. *Noise: A Flaw in Human Judgment.* Little, Brown Spark, 2021.

Klingberg, Torkel. *The Overflowing Brain: Information Overload and the Limits of Working Memory.* Oxford University Press, 2008.

Kofman, Fred. *Conscious Business: How to Build Value Through Values.* 2nd edition. Sounds True, 2013.

Lakoff, George. *Women, Fire, and Dangerous Things: What Categories Reveal About the Mind.* University of Chicago Press, 1990.

Levitin, Daniel J. *The Organized Mind: Thinking Straight in the Age of Information Overload.* Dutton, 2014.

Lewis, Jason. *The War for Fundraising Talent: And How Small Shops Can Win.* Gatekeeper Press, 2018.

LiveScience.com. "Why We Remember Traumatic Events Better," July 26, 2005.

Lustig, Robert. *The Hacking of the American Mind: The Science Behind the Corporate Takeover of Our Bodies and Brains.* Avery, 2018.

Napper, Paul, and Anthony Rao. *The Power of Agency: The 7 Principles to Conquer Obstacles, Make Effective Decisions, and Create a Life on Your Own Terms.* St. Martin's Press, 2019.

Newport, Cal. *Deep Work: Rules for Focused Success in a Distracted World.* Grand Central Publishing, 2016.

Olson, David L. "Software Process Simulation." In *Encyclopedia of Information Systems*, edited by H. Bidgoli. Vol. 2 (pp. 143–153). Academic Press, 2003.

Parker, Priya. *The Art of Gathering: How We Meet and Why It Matters.* International edition, Riverhead Books, 2018.

Passaro, John A. *6 Minutes Wrestling with Life.* Blurb, 2016.

Paulos, John Allen. *Innumeracy: Mathematical Illiteracy and Its Consequences.* Collins Publishers, 1988.

Rosenberg, Marshall B. *Nonviolent Communication: A Language of Life.* 2nd edition. PuddleDancer, 2003.

Ryan, J. E. *Wait, What?: And Life's Other Essential Questions.* HarperOne, 2017.

Tavris, Carol, and Elliot Aronson. *Mistakes Were Made (but Not by Me): Why We Justify Foolish Beliefs, Bad Decisions, and Hurtful Acts*. 3rd ed. Mariner Books, 2015.

Urban, Andrew. *The Nonprofit Buyer: Strategies for Success from a Nonprofit Technology Sales Veteran*. CreateSpace Independent Publishing, 2010.

Wilber, K., Patten, T., Leonard, A., and Morelli, M. *Integral Life Practice: A 21st-Century Blueprint for Physical Health, Emotional Balance, Mental Clarity, and Spiritual Awakening* (illustrated edition). Integral Books, 2018.

Yates, John, Matthew Immergut, and Jeremy Graves. *The Mind Illuminated: A Complete Meditation Guide Integrating Buddhist Wisdom and Brain Science for Greater Mindfulness*. Touchstone, 2017.

Acknowledgments

WE WANT TO thank the people who help remind us daily about what matters, and fill our lives with joy. Chris's amazing wife, Erica, and two awesome kids, Elaine and Sam, bring an amazing amount of joy. Chris lost his beloved father, Barry Cannon, in 2021, which heightened his focus on seizing the day, every day. Daily inspiration for Michael comes from his incredible wife, Rachael, and wonderful sons, Lucas and Evan. Michael is lucky to have parents and in-laws, extended family, and friends who infuse his days with joy. The luxury of being able to write this book was largely due to the support and encouragement of so many loved ones.

We are also grateful for the support and backing of our teams at Zuri Group and Yale's alumni affairs and development office. Dozens of other colleagues and professionals played a hand in getting us to focus on this book. Our featured interviewees—Blaire Atkinson, Amy Bobrick, Chris Campbell, Nathan Chappell, Jay Dillon, Dwight Dozier, Cara Giacomini, Kent Grove, Joe Manok, Camden Morse, Brent Grinna, David Nolan, Art Ochoa, Brittany Shaff, and Travis Soyer—made the book clearer and more relevant. Hawken Brackett contributed his ideas and crucial edits to the book. Jocelyn Kane gave us impactful and clarifying edits throughout. Many others offered advice or ideas along the way. We should thank our industry mentors and colleagues whose insights shaped our thinking. Cynthia Holter, Steve Wilkerson, Jeff Huntington, Robin Krajaulis, Don Whelan, Paul Schnabel, Josh Birkholz, Mark Marshall, Katrina Klaproth, John Murphy, Howard Horowitz, Stephanie Burnett, Molly Graham, Ken Swift, Kate Nimety, Brandon Ferris, and Chris's other superb Zuri colleagues have made a huge impact on this book and the nonprofit space. None of this would have been possible without the steadfast support of Joan O'Neill, vice president of alumni affairs and development at Yale, and Sondra Cruver, senior director of information and donor services, and the advancement systems, advancement technology and IMDS teams, as well as far, far too many Yale colleagues to name. Likewise, all of our Causativity friends and advisers, especially Reggie Solomon, Eamonn Edge, Lauren Summers, and Sean McAvoy, as well as Umi Howard, Tim Stringer, Lisa Kimmel, Danielle Casioppo, David Gumpert, Alan Fine, and Jen Cinque gave much-needed encouragement and support. Meredith Fahey, who passed away in September 2020, continues to be a light for us. For mindfulness ideas, special thanks to Anne Dutton, Dana Foster, Loren Sterman (and other friends at TBT), and far too many fellow mindfulness practitioners to name. Others across the nonprofit industry, colleagues like Rob Scott, Karl Otto, Dayle Matchett, Chris Speier, Paul Lucht, Jimmy Aldridge, Theresa Pesch, Michael McClintick, Cassie Hunt, Beth Zapatka, Martha Callaghan, Jocelyn Kane, Cindy Mariani, Monty Shepardson, Mark Walcott and Tori Rysz, have focused us through their own leadership and thinking. Our Wiley colleagues, Brian Neill, Linda Brandon, Deborah Schindlar, and the rest of that expert group, made this publication a breeze. A special thank-you goes to Hannah Lewis, whose design skills mightily improved this book's visual appeal.

And, finally, we need to thank you, the reader, for choosing *Focused Fundraising*. We appreciate the irony of writing about overload with the risk of overloading you. We trust the focus this will bring in your work and life made the read worthwhile.

Index